COMMUNITY SERVICE FOR TEEN

EXPANDING EDUCATION & LITERACY
OPPORTUNITIES TO VOLUNTEER

by Bernard Ryan, Jr.

361.37
RY9

Ryan, Bernard, 1923-
   Community service for teens: opportunities to volunteer / Bernard Ryan, Jr.
   p. cm.
   Includes bibliographical references and index.
   Contents: [1] Caring for animals -- [2] Expanding education and literacy -- [3] Helping the ill, the poor & the elderly -- [4] Increasing neighborhood service -- [5] Participating in government -- -[6] Promoting the arts and sciences -- [7] Protecting the environment - -[8] Serving with police, fire & EMS
   ISBN 0-89434-227-4 (v. 1). -- ISBN 0-89434-231-2 (v. 2). -- ISBN 0-89434-229-0 (v. 3). -- ISBN 0-89434-233-9 (v. 4). -- ISBN 0-89434-230-4 (v. 5). -- ISBN 0-89434-234-7 (v. 6). -- ISBN 0-89434-228-2 (v. 7). -- ISBN 0-89434-232-0 (v. 8)
   1. Voluntarism—United States—Juvenile literature. 2. Young volunteers—United States—Juvenile literature. 3. Teenage volunteers in social service—United States—Juvenile literature.
[1. Voluntarism.] I. Title.
HN90.V64R93 1998
361.3'7'08350973—dc21
                                                         97-34971
                                                             CIP
                                                              AC

Community Service for Teens: Expanding Education and Literacy: Opportunities to Volunteer

A New England Publishing Associates Book
Copyright ©1998 by Ferguson Publishing Company
ISBN 0-89434-231-2

Published and distributed by
Ferguson Publishing Company
200 West Madison, Suite 300
Chicago, Illinois 60606
800-306-9941
Web Site: http://www.fergpubco.com

All Rights Reserved. This book may not be duplicated in any way without the express permission of the publisher, except in the form of brief excerpts or quotations for the purpose of review. The information contained herein is for the personal use of the reader and may not be incorporated in any commercial programs, other books, databases or any kind of software without the written consent of the publisher. Making copies of this book or any portion for any purpose other than your own is a violation of United States copyright laws.

Printed in the United States of America
V-3

CONTENTS

Introduction 5
1. What Are Education and Literacy? 10
2. What You'll Do as a Volunteer 21
3. What It Takes to Work in Education and Literacy 45
4. What's in It for You? 58
5. Is It Right for You? 71
6. Where to Find Opportunities 83
Glossary 89
Suggestions for Further Reading 91
Index 94

INTRODUCTION

Six out of ten American teenagers work as volunteers. A 1996 survey revealed that the total number of teen volunteers aged 12 to 17 is 13.3 million. They give 2.4 billion hours each year. Of that time, 1.8 billion hours are spent in "formal" commitments to nonprofit organizations. Informal help, like "just helping neighbors," receives 600 million hours.

Each "formal" volunteer gives an average of three and a half hours a week. It would take nearly 1.1 million full-time employees to match these hours. And if the formal volunteers were paid minimum wage for their time, the cost would come to at least $7.7 billion—a tremendous saving to nonprofit organizations.

Teen volunteerism is growing. In the four years between the 1996 survey and a previous one, the number of volunteers grew by 7 percent and their hours increased by 17 percent.

Equal numbers of girls and boys give their time to volunteering.

How voluntary is volunteering? Only 16 out of 100 volunteers go to schools that insist on community service before graduation. Twenty-six out of 100 are in schools that offer courses requiring community service if you want credit for the course.

Six out of ten teen volunteers started volunteering before they were 14 years old. Seventy-eight percent of teens who volunteer have parents who volunteer.

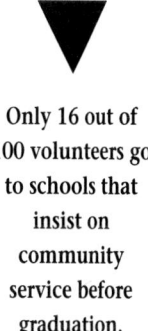

Only 16 out of 100 volunteers go to schools that insist on community service before graduation.

WHY VOLUNTEER?

When teens are asked to volunteer, the 1996 survey revealed, nine out of ten do so. Who does the asking? Usually a friend, teacher,

◀ EXPANDING EDUCATION & LITERACY: OPPORTUNITIES TO VOLUNTEER ▶

(Courtesy: Community Action for Greater Middletown, Middletown, CT)

Opportunities for teen volunteers exist with many nonprofit organizations. Head Start, a child development program, sponsors summer programs encouraging teens to work with children. Teacher Terry Smith and volunteer Heather Persico have fun with kids on a hot summer day.

family member, or church member. Teens gave a number of reasons for volunteering, regardless of whether their schools required community service. Their reasons included:

- You feel compassion for people in need.
- You feel you can do something for a cause that is important to you.
- You believe that if you help others, others will help you.
- Your volunteering is important to people you respect.
- You learn to relate to others who may be different from you.

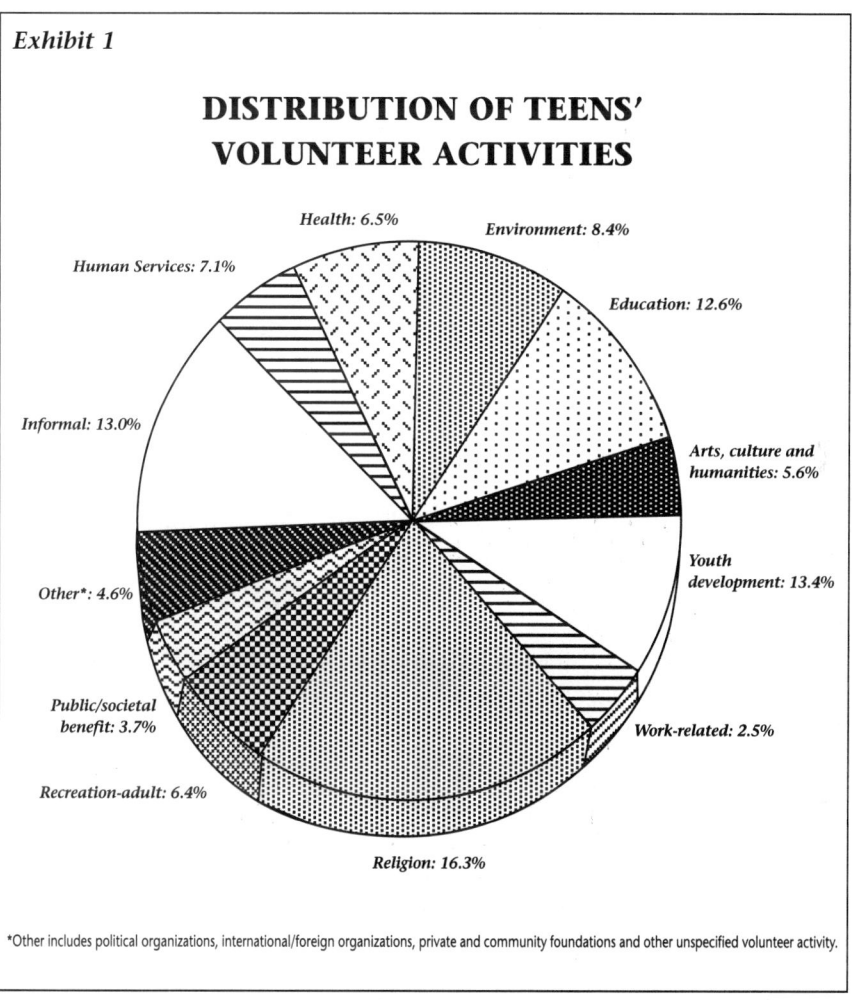

(Source: Volunteering and Giving Among American Teenagers: 1996. Independent Sector, Washington, D.C., 1997.)

- You develop leadership skills.
- You become more patient.
- You gain a better understanding of good citizenship.
- You get a chance to learn about various careers.
- You gain experience that can help in school and can lead to college admission and college scholarships as well as future careers.

VOLUNTEER FOR WHAT?

You can volunteer in a wide variety of activities. To get a picture of how teen volunteering is spread among various categories, see Exhibit 1.

WHO SAYS YOU HAVE TO "VOLUNTEER"?

Is "volunteering" for community service required in your school? It is if you live in the state of Maryland or in the city of Atlanta, Georgia. In fact, in many school districts across the United States you cannot receive your high school diploma unless you have spent a certain number of hours in community service. The number of hours varies.

Who makes the rule? In Maryland, the only state so far to require every high school student to perform community service, it is the Maryland State Department of Education. In most school districts, it is the board of education, which usually sets policies that meet the standards of the community.

If you have to do it, is it voluntary? And is it legal to make you do it? One family didn't think so. In 1994, the parents of Daniel Immediato, a 17-year-old senior at Rye Neck High School in Mamaroneck, New York, sued in federal court to keep Daniel's school from requiring him to spend 40 hours in community service before he could graduate.

Daniel's parents said the requirement interfered with their right to raise their child, that it violated Daniel's privacy rights, and that it was a violation of the Thirteenth Amendment to the U. S. Constitution.

(Continued on page 9)

(Continued from page 8)

That amendment says:

> Neither slavery nor involuntary servitude, except as a punishment for a crime whereof the party shall have been duly convicted, shall exist within the United States, or any place subject to their jurisdiction.

The requirement for community service, said the Immediatos, imposed involuntary servitude on Daniel.

In its defense, the Rye Neck School Board argued that what it wanted was to get the students out into the community to see what goes on in the outside world. In the process, said the board, students would find out what it was like to have to dress appropriately for a job, be on time somewhere and have other people dependent on them. The emphasis was not on what the community would gain, it was on what the student would learn.

The court decided the school system was right. The Immediatos appealed. The U.S. Court of Appeals for the Second Circuit upheld the decision. The Immediatos asked the U.S. Supreme Court to hear the case. It turned down the request, as it does many appeals, without stating its reason for refusing.

CHAPTER ONE

What Are Education and Literacy?

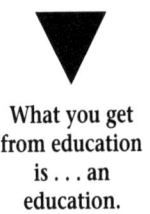

What you get from education is . . . an education.

*W*e all know the word *education*. But we don't often think about the vast world it covers. We don't use the word *literacy* as often. Yet it relates closely to education. Each word is a kind of idea that you cannot carry with you—except inside your brain. Each is an abstraction. Each offers you many opportunities to serve your community.

EDUCATION: A PROCESS AND ITS RESULT

Think of education as a process—something that goes on and on. But think of it also as the result of the process. What you get from education is . . . an education. Sounds funny, but it's true. Education is the system through which you gain all your knowledge as well as the skills you need to get through life. And that's not to mention the values and attitudes toward life that you pick up along the way.

The process has two sides: *formal education* and *informal education.*

Formal Education

You get formal education in schools and colleges. In America, you are entitled by law in every state to go to public school free of charge from grades 1 through 12. Many public school systems include kinder-

(Courtesy: Community Action for Greater Middletown, Middletown, CT)

The Head Start program began in 1965 to help meet the emotional, social, nutritional and psychological needs of preschool children from low-income families. Teen volunteer Jennifer Ortiz helps a little girl with her face-painting at an Easter party.

garten, the year before first grade, and many also include Head Start, which accepts kids younger than kindergarten age.

In most states, you are not only entitled, you are required to go to school until you reach a certain age—usually 16. Some states and local communities, however, permit "home study," in which you are taught by your parents or others at home, although you must pass state tests regularly.

Education involves more people than any other single effort in our country. One-fourth of all Americans are students and teachers—in the mid-1990s, 62 million people went to school or college and nearly 4 million did the teaching.

What is education trying to do to you—and for you? It helps you deal with your world by teaching you in three basic areas. They are *cognitive, affective,* and *psychomotor.*

Education involves more people than any other single effort in our country.

The Cognitive Area. This describes your thinking process. It is where you store information, build up knowledge and figure things out. It is what you use to solve problems.

Who are your teachers in this area? In most cases, they are the professional teachers. They are trained in the most effective ways to help you in school.

The Affective Area. This is where you put your feelings. It is where you know right from wrong. Here you appreciate music and art, poetry and rainbows. Your spiritual side lies here, along with your moral values and emotions. Character building occurs in this department. This is where your interest in community service hangs its hat.

Your teachers in this area are your schoolteachers, your parents and siblings and other relatives, as well as your minister, priest, rabbi or other religious leader. Your friends—peers, or older or younger friends—also have an influence here.

The Psychomotor Area. This part of education is where you park your mechanical and muscular abilities. Throwing a baseball, performing a pirouette, riding a bicycle, drawing a cartoon, changing a tire—all are psychomotor skills. Some, such as handwriting and drawing and the athletic skills that come under physical education, you learn in formal education. You learn many other skills in informal education.

WHAT ARE EDUCATION AND LITERACY?

(V. Harlow)

Informal education includes many activities outside the classroom. These baseball players are working together as a team toward a common goal, and the praise they receive for a "win" is part of their reward.

In this area, your teachers are the professionals you see in school every day as well as your coaches, your parents and siblings, and your peers.

Informal Education

In a sense, informal education includes everything you learn outside of school. It is the knowledge you acquire at home, at church, on the baseball diamond, football or soccer field, hockey rink or ski slope, at the ballet barre, watching TV or listening to the radio, reading newspapers and magazines, in the Girl Scouts or Boy Scouts. It may include activities that occur in school—the drama club, the 4-H Club, the glee club, for instance—but never demand that you write a paper or take an exam.

HOW DO YOU LEARN?

▼

You learn by forming mental habits.

No one has yet figured out *exactly* how we learn. But psychologists have worked out three basic theories of learning, and they generally agree that most people's learning process involves all three. The basic theories are: behavior modification, cognitive or problem solving, and humanistic.

Behavior Modification Theory

This theory is also known as *stimulus-response.* The idea is that you learn by forming mental habits. You make it a habit of recognizing that 5 x 5 = 25. You make it a habit of tossing a basketball through the hoop. When you are asked, "How much is five times five?" and you answer, "Twenty-five," or when you sink the ball through the basket, you get praised. If you miss the basket or respond with the wrong number, you get corrected. The praise is nice and rewarding, so you form the habit of doing or saying the right thing.

Cognitive or Problem-solving Theory

The behavior modification theory works fine when there is only one correct answer. But suppose you come up with more than one solution to a problem. Then you have to figure out relationships and decide which is the most effective solution.

In this kind of learning, your teacher doesn't just praise you when you are right and correct you when you are wrong. Rather, your teacher asks questions and guides you to information that helps you discover all the possible solutions. You then decide which is best.

Humanistic Theory

Some psychologists think that the behavior modification and the cognitive theories both ignore your emotional development. Since no two people have the same personality, they say, you should be allowed to develop in your own way.

Under this theory, your teacher helps you explore your emotional needs and desires, and then steers you toward knowledge and skills that meet them. For your life to be satisfying, according to the humanistic theory, you must be given challenging activities in which you make your own decisions. The term *creativity* is often associated with this process. Creativity simply means that you put your imagination to work with information and skills you have already learned, with the result that you bring something into being or make something happen.

General Rules of Learning

If you want some general rules about learning, think about these:
1. Within a given amount of practice time, you can usually learn a task more easily if you work in short practice sessions spaced widely apart, instead of longer sessions held closer together.
2. You can learn many tasks best by imitating experts.
3. You should perform a new activity yourself, rather than just watching or listening to someone.
4. You learn better if you know immediately how good your performance was.
5. You should practice difficult parts of a task separately and then try to incorporate them into the task as a whole.[2]

[2] *The World Book Encyclopedia,* E Volume 6. Chicago: World Book, Inc., 1996, p. 96.

Think about these rules as you get involved in any of the volunteer activities described in chapters 2 and 3—or, for example, if you are learning a foreign language, the game of tennis or how to drive a car.

LITERACY AND ILLITERACY

You are *literate* if you know how to read and write. You are *illiterate* if you can do neither. You are *functionally illiterate* if you cannot read or write well enough to handle everyday activities, such as filling out an application for a job, balancing a checkbook, or reading a street sign, telephone book or directions on a package.

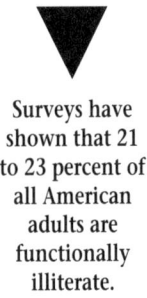

Surveys have shown that 21 to 23 percent of all American adults are functionally illiterate.

Many Americans are functionally illiterate. Large numbers dropped out of school before completing the eighth grade. A great many others were given "social promotion" through the elementary grades and high school, even though their teachers knew they were functionally illiterate. Why? Because the authorities wanted to save them from the embarrassment of being held back with younger students.

Surveys, some going back 20 years or more, have shown that 21 to 23 percent of all American adults are functionally illiterate. That's 40 to 44 million adults. Among English-speaking Americans aged 23 to 25, 16 percent are functionally illiterate. And the statistics show that illiteracy in America is increasing.

Here's another startling fact: 15 million adults who hold jobs are functionally illiterate. In fact, many large corporations have installed basic courses in reading and writing for new employees who could not read simple instructions and how-to manuals. Three-quarters of the Fortune 500 companies provide remedial literacy training for their employees. And among the unemployed, according to the U.S. Department of Education, 6 out of 10 lack the basic skills they need to be trained for high-tech jobs.

The U.S. Department of Education has set up projects to improve the teaching of reading and writing in public schools. Several private nonprofit organizations have gone to work on the problem. They offer programs to help adults catch up on reading and writing skills they missed when they were young. They also work with schools to help establish these skills in the elementary grades.

This is where you come in. Two of the most successful private organizations—Literacy Volunteers of America and Laubach Literacy Action—use teenagers as tutors. Each recruits and trains volunteers to teach the illiterate how to read and write. In other chapters of this book, you will meet some of their teenage tutors and some of the people who coordinate their work. Through them, you will find out how you can help.

Reading is the primary route for the delivery of information from somewhere else into your brain.

READING: WHAT IS IT?

Reading is how you get information into your head from printed or written words. The words can be anywhere—on your computer screen, in a book, on a sign or in a newspaper or magazine. You recognize letters, individually or in groups. You know they represent sounds that form words. The words represent ideas. (You also get information into your head from listening and from direct observation. But reading is the primary route for the delivery of information from somewhere else into your brain. Reading is fundamental to our civilization. In fact, wherever you go around the world, the countries that boast the most advanced technology, science and economy are those that have the highest percentages of literacy.)

As you know, when you learn words you build your vocabulary. The more words you know, the more *comprehensive* your reading— if you have learned the meanings of the words. Comprehension is understanding. It is what all teachers of reading are after.

Think of reading comprehension as a process. To read with comprehension, you apply the knowledge and the experience you already have to the words you are reading. You could not be reading

◄ EXPANDING EDUCATION & LITERACY: OPPORTUNITIES TO VOLUNTEER ►

(Courtesy: Patricia Heck/Club RIF, Red Mountain High School, Mesa, AZ)

Much of the information you need to work and function on a daily basis is available only in printed form. That makes reading the most fundamental skill you must have in today's society.

this book if you had not already learned how to do that.

But many young children, especially if they have lived in underprivileged families or neighborhoods, do not have a broad base of experience. They have had little informative conversation. Stimulating ideas have not come their way. The value of printed materials is lost on them. Such children need a jump start. They need older tutors—people like you—as well as their professional teachers, to read *to* them and (maybe even more important) to read along *with* them.

HAVING A BIG PERSON TO LOOK UP TO

"It's really just spending time with them and reading with them," says Meaghan Kennedy, a teen volunteer at Red Mountain High School in Mesa, Arizona.

As a Club RIF (Reading Is Fundamental) member, Meaghan is allowed to leave her school during a free period three times a week so she can work with first- and second-graders. "I read stories to the children and I help them with different subjects that they might be having trouble with," she says.

"I also just play with them a lot and spend time with them, because they really like to have a big person all to themselves to look up to," Meaghan notes.

TEACHING: WHAT IS IT?

No profession in the world has more members than teaching. The United States has 3.75 million teachers. Most of them follow four basic procedures:

1. *Getting ready.* Before class begins, your teacher decides on a daily lesson plan. This fits the curriculum set by your school board or administration for the class.
2. *Directing learning.* Using textbooks, audiovisuals and other materials, the teacher guides you—either individually or in a group—in step-by-step procedures for mastering whatever subject you are studying.
3. *Testing progress.* Your teacher has to know how you are coming along. Oral and written tests help the teacher discover who needs help, and what kind of help to give.
4. *Keeping records and advising.* Teachers must maintain the school's records on attendance. Student papers must be reviewed and marked. Hobby clubs and extracurricular activities need advisers. Teams need coaches. And many students can use individual counseling on personal matters as well as the academics.

Altogether, teaching is a 24-hour-a-day, 7-day-a-week profession. Most teachers love it. Some become cynical. Some burn out. All welcome help.

The help can come from paid teacher's aides or paraprofessionals, if the school can afford them. It can also come from volunteers, such as parents who serve as room mothers and fathers or in other jobs.

As you will see in the chapters to come, you can help teachers, too. You can become a student volunteer and help your peers or the younger kids in the elementary grades.

CHAPTER TWO

What You'll Do as a Volunteer

*W*hat types of work can you do as a volunteer? The range is from helping within the walls of your own school building, to volunteering in public libraries, to giving your time in the broader community. And the people you can help range in age from preschool to your peers to senior citizens.

IN THE PUBLIC LIBRARY

As a volunteer in your public library, you can help in several ways. One is with the basic housekeeping. Cartloads of books that have been returned by borrowers have to be sorted. They must be put back on the shelves, in precisely the right places, so they can be found easily and loaned again. New books must be marked and put into the computer catalog—a job you may or may not be asked to help with, depending on your computer skills and the librarians' attitudes toward teen volunteers.

In any library, someone must replenish the supplies of pencils and scrap paper. Someone must refill the copying machines with paper. Someone must hunt down missing or misplaced books and cassettes. You can be that someone—one who takes responsibility for the little jobs that have to be done. By doing them, you give the librarians more time to do their professional work for the library's patrons.

A public library works hard to encourage young children to discover the joy of reading. It schedules story times for preschool children. If

◀ EXPANDING EDUCATION & LITERACY: OPPORTUNITIES TO VOLUNTEER ▶

(V. Harlow/Russell Library, Middletown, CT)

When you volunteer at a public library, you may be asked to put books back on the shelves after borrowers have returned them.

story time is on a weekday during the school year, you cannot help because you are in school yourself. But if it is on Saturday, you can volunteer to help with it.

During the summer months, you can be an active volunteer in your library's summer reading club. Usually kids from kindergarten to fifth grade belong to the club. They come into the library to report on books they are reading or have completed. You help them record their progress in a reading log. You ask them questions about what they have read. In some clubs, you play games with them.

A READING PROGRAM THAT'S A HIT

"Over the summer," says Janice Kochanov, a teen volunteer at the Danbury (Connecticut) Public Library, "we run a contest to get kids interested in reading.

"We have two teams, the orange and the blue, and the game has a baseball theme. Each child gets a board shaped like a baseball diamond. After they've read a few books, we ask them questions so we know whether they read the books. We do that for each book. Then we stamp the baseball board. When they get enough stamps to get to first base, they get a prize—a pencil, or eraser, or free ice cream. They get more prizes as they go around the diamond. When they get to home plate, they get a medal and we put their picture in the library. So they really get rewarded all along the way."

And there are other library jobs. You can help fill out name tags for the children who come in for story time.

The library is sure to have some special programs—readings by guest authors, for example, or a play or skit that you and other teen volunteers put on. You can set up seating areas and refreshment tables, pass out tickets, help with the ushering, serve the refreshments and make yourself useful answering questions. And you can help clean up after the crowd goes home.

◄ EXPANDING EDUCATION & LITERACY: OPPORTUNITIES TO VOLUNTEER ►

All of this frees up the librarians to help other people find books and information.

In the Summer Reading Club, we work from nine to twelve every morning for a full week. Every volunteer gets assigned to a certain week, and you do it with a couple of other kids. You can come in and do more if you like, but not with the others—you help sort books and do other jobs.
        —Teen Volunteer Autumn Weir,
      Danbury, Connecticut, Public Library

SCHOOL PROGRAMS

There are many volunteer opportunities right within your school system. Some activities to consider are:
- Club RIF
- tutoring
- Head Start
- peer leadership and counseling

Club RIF

For more than 30 years, an organization called Reading Is Fundamental (RIF) has been working to help children become strong readers. Headquartered in Washington, D.C., RIF operates in all 50 states and the U.S. territories. Its projects are local, at about 17,000 different "sites" or communities. Some 74 percent of the sites are in schools. Others are located in day-care centers, libraries and other places such as Head Start centers. Over the years, RIF has put 175 million new books into the hands, and the homes, of American children. By giving away books and running programs that encourage the desire to read, it serves 3.74 million children every year.

(Courtesy: Patricia Heck/Club RIF, Red Mountain High School, Mesa, AZ)

Reading is Fundamental (RIF), an organization that encourages children to become strong readers, has 17,000 sites throughout the United States. This RIF volunteer reads to a group of youngsters at Red Mountain High School, in Mesa, Arizona.

Because its projects are local, Reading Is Fundamental has an opportunity for you. It welcomes teen volunteers. To see what you might be doing as a volunteer, look at Club RIF in Red Mountain High School in Mesa, Arizona. This Club RIF has some 600 teenage members. If you were a member, you might be doing any of the following. Think of the first two as teaching activities. The others are key jobs that bring in the funds, carry on the extensive program of book donations, and enlist new members to replace those who graduate from school.

    1. *Tutoring.* At a nearby elementary school, you tutor kids from first to sixth grade, three times a week. Usually the teacher

has worked out tutoring needs in math, spelling or reading. For two of the three days, you concentrate on the assigned tutoring. You also grade papers and give spelling tests.

2. *Reading.* On the third day, you do reading exercises, following a lesson plan that goes with the storybook you are using. You may be one of the readers in the "Reading Buddies" program. Here you read one-on-one with younger children, usually in the second grade—the grade that is crucial for catching on to reading.

CHOOSING THE RIGHT BOOKS TO READ

"It's really important to pick things at their level," says Club RIF teen volunteer Meaghan Kennedy.

Meaghan likes to take her own favorite books to read with first- and second-graders. "One of the favorites of all the kids," she says, "is *Where the Wild Things Are* by Maurice Sendak. They all love that story. It's important that you read the children age-appropriate books. If the stories are too long or if they don't have enough fun things in them, the kids won't understand or get into them. So it's really important to pick things at their level."

3. *Giving books.* Club RIF gives new books to the community—placing them in homeless shelters, in other schools and in the homes of children in disadvantaged neighborhoods, ranging from inner-city to rural. Where does it get the books? Many are donated. And the club buys otherswith money it gets by putting on fund-raisers. The Red Mountain High School club gives away 20,000 books each year.

ORGANIZE A BOOK DRIVE

"We get books donated from bookstores across the country," says Brandy Grant, a Club RIF teen volunteer at Red Mountain High School in Mesa, Arizona. "We have to get a lot of them donated because we don't have funds to buy them. Then we take a bus out to an Indian community. All the kids are gathered together and we have a big distribution. Each child can pick out two or three books. We also read with them, and work with them to see what level their skills are at. And we encourage the parents to read to their children at home."

4. *Raising funds.* You can help run a number of fund-raising events throughout the school year. Many clubs have raised money through car washes, candy sales, shows and skits put on at school.

5. *Recruiting.* Every high school organization must keep bringing in new members as seniors graduate. As a Club RIF member, you work hard not only to increase the love of reading but also to expand the group's membership. You help put on special school assemblies about reading. You mount hallway displays emphasizing the Reading Is Fundamental theme.

We promote positive reading attitudes from all different directions. At our high school assembly on reading, we invite 150 second-graders over to be a part of it. The whole assembly is about reading, with 500 kids involved.
—Sponsor Patricia Heck, Club RIF,
Red Mountain High School, Mesa, Arizona

(Courtesy: Patricia Heck/Club RIF, Red Mountain High School, Mesa, AZ)

Current Club RIF members in Mesa, Arizona, take time out from their activities to recruit new members at a local junior high shool.

Tutoring

Many elementary-school children have no one at home until 5:00 P.M. or even later. So schools offer after-school programs beginning when school gets out at about 3:30. And some of these children need tutoring help. This gives you an opportunity to spend about an hour and a half, from one to five days a week, helping kids in grades one through five.

Suppose you go to tutor at such a school. When you get there, you will probably help first with snack time and a brief recess marking the end of the formal school day. Then you'll turn to a folder of homework that the teacher has prepared for, say, a second-grader. Usually you work one-on-one with the same student for several sessions, but sometimes you may find that the teacher wants you to work with three or four students together.

A LESSON IN ORGANIZING

"Each teacher organizes the work into folders. The goal is for the students to spend the most time on something they need the most help with," says Sara Copetto, a teen tutor at Children's Community School in Waterbury, Connecticut.

"In each folder the teacher has a paper that outlines the work inside. For example, the teacher might instruct us to spend the first 15 minutes reading with the child and the next 20 minutes doing a math ditto," explains Sara. "The time is broken up pretty well. We try and get everything in. The girl I work with has more problems in English than in math, so we do a lot of reading."

(Continued on page 30)

> *(Continued from page 29)*
>
> On each of three days a week, Melva Jones spends an hour and a half helping second- and third-graders at the Children's Community School. "The teachers tell us if they want us to spend more time on reading, or if they want us to spend more time on spelling or on math," she says. "We might work on counting, by threes or twos or tens or fives. The boy I work with has this book called 'specific skills,' where they ask him questions and he has to comprehend what they are asking him and then answer questions about that. The directions might be, circle the word that goes with the phrase at the end. And then the question would be, 'The directions ask you to circle it, underline it, or cross it out.' And then he'll circle it. So he's got to know which one it means. And that shows his comprehension."

Head Start

Head Start is a U.S. government program that helps preschool-age children from economically disadvantaged neighborhoods get ready to start school. Its centers are operated locally, either in school buildings or in such places as community centers. Usually the summer months are its busiest times.

Head Start depends on volunteers. Many parents of the children in the program help out. If you join the thousands of teen volunteers across the country who help at Head Start centers, you will be introducing three- and four-year-olds to a wide range of activities.

The Head Start program is designed to spur children's growth in many ways—socially, emotionally, intellectually and physically. You

WHAT YOU'LL DO AS A VOLUNTEER

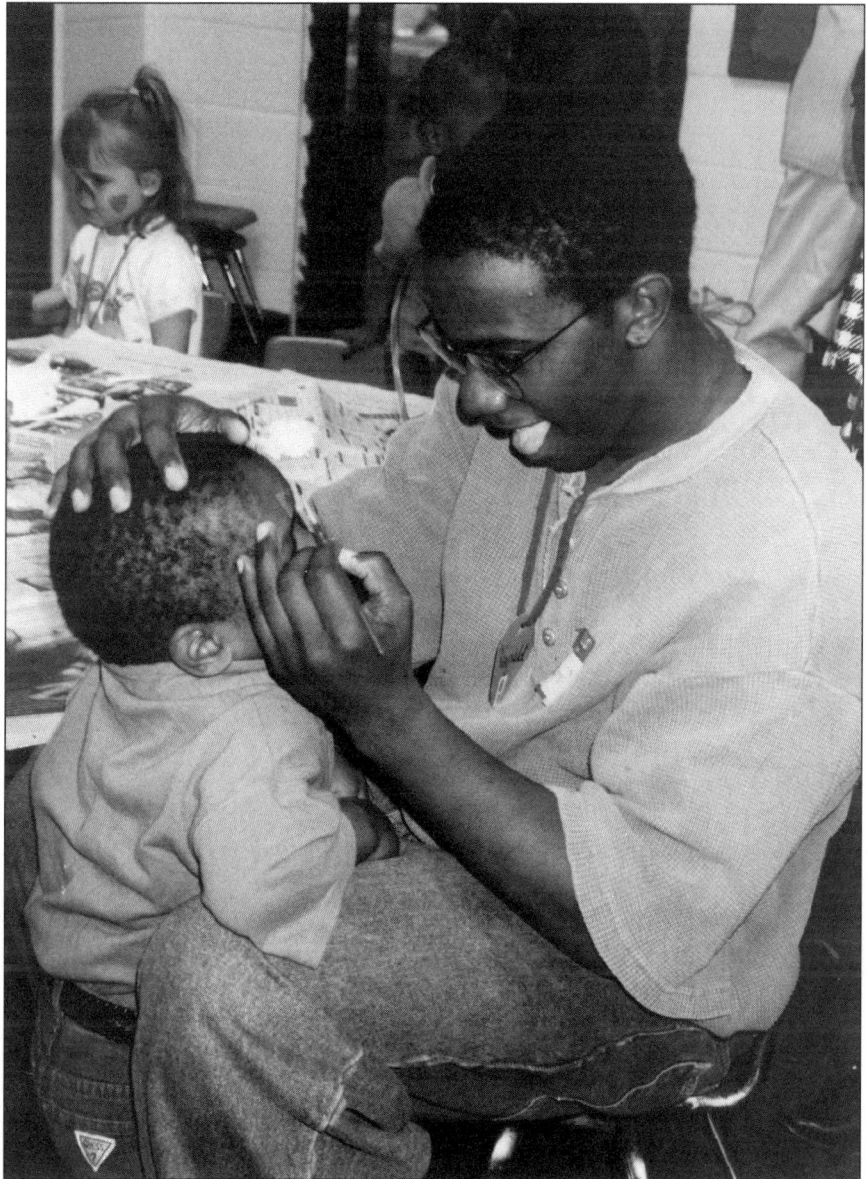

(Courtesy: Community Action for Greater Middletown, Middletown, CT)

The Head Start program depends on volunteers, especially with younger children for whom "formal instruction" may be replaced with other important skills such as social or physical activities. Jukorie Davis, a Head Start volunteer in Middletown, Connecticut, paints a preschooler's face at an Easter party.

won't be teaching or tutoring in the strict sense, because the kids are too little for "formal" instruction. But they will be learning from you as you help them gain skills you take for granted—such as language and literacy, cognitive ability and social development. The "curriculum" you participate in, for perhaps two hours a day for a couple of days a week, will include field trips (to firehouses, recycling plants, stores and parks), plenty of singing and dancing and simple science experiments and demonstrations.

DOING THE LITTLE THINGS THAT HELP

"Most of our volunteering by teens is done in our Head Start program," says Ellen Block, coordinator of volunteers for Lenox Hill Neighborhood House in New York City.

"The teens assist the teacher and the assistant teacher. They do things like put the blocks away, read to a child and so on. They do all kinds of little things that help," notes Block. "The only students who can volunteer for the Head Start program during the school year are those whose schools give them release time. The student volunteers have to be available when our Head Start schools are open," she explains.

Peer Leadership and Counseling

Another group of students you can help educate is the one with you in high school—either in your grade level or, if you are a junior or senior, a grade or two below you.

Peer leadership. The Chain Reaction Youth Leadership Program is a major national program that helps teen volunteers learn how to talk to their peers. Sponsored by the March of Dimes Birth Defects Foundation, the program operates in some 35 communities across the United States and is organizing still more. In Chain Reaction, you develop such skills as public speaking, marketing, meeting planning and goal setting—and you help your peers to develop these skills, too.

Take Ann Futterknecht as an example. She joined Chain Reaction while she was in high school in Gainesville, Florida. Ann became team captain for her school for the annual WalkAmerica. She made presentations to school clubs, faculty meetings and classes, explaining why WalkAmerica is important to them and why they should support the March of Dimes. She set the fund-raising goals for her school, developed a plan to meet the goals and organized Chain Reaction members to work on the campaign.

We held retreats where we did the planning and goal setting . . . and helped educate the new members on what the mission is. And then we did some health education stuff, where you're a speaker during a workshop about what you can do to prevent birth defects, what birth defects are, and some health issues in general.
—**Ann Futterknecht, chairman,
Chain Reaction National Youth Council**

In her Sioux Falls, South Dakota, high school, Kristen Moore was in charge of special projects in the Chain Reaction Youth Leadership Council. According to Kristen, her job was "to take on new ideas and put them into blueprints."

One of the ideas Kristen's group put into action was holding conferences. "We put on a big youth leadership conference," she explains. "We wanted to help kids learn about the skills they'll need for college and later on. We invited students from four major high schools—from members of the teams, the music groups, the debaters, all different areas. In previous years we've had conferences on issues like drugs and alcohol."

Still other in-school conferences organized and run by Chain Reaction teen volunteers include nutrition, management of time, teen pregnancy, and AIDS.

I'm a peer minister. You could say that's sort of a spiritual thing. We volunteer to help the freshmen in the school get acclimated to their environment.
—Melva Jones, high school volunteer,
Waterbury, Connecticut

Peer counseling. Some people have a natural ability to lend a sympathetic ear and come up with commonsense advice. If you are that kind of person, you may want to volunteer in a group called Natural Peer Helpers. What you do is quiet, behind-the-scenes work, because almost all of it is highly confidential. You are dealing with situations that are known only to those immediately involved.

"It's mentoring to the entire school community," says Abbie Allanach, a Natural Peer Helper in Connecticut. "We handle everything from small problems between friends or teachers and students all the way to family problems like divorce and even suicide—any sort of concern that someone might have. As a Peer Helper, we normally start off just listening to the person's problem, and sometimes that's all we have to do. All that people need sometimes is just someone to listen to them.

"We never give advice. Instead, we try to help the person come to their own conclusions about the problem. We try to restate the problem for them, so they see it in a different light. We try to help them analyze the situation so they can help themselves—so they can go on and make their own decisions as to how they should act.

"In a situation where someone is depressed or is contemplating suicide, we try to help them see what is good about their life. We try to help them look again at things that give their life value—that's what you forget about when you're in a state of depression. That's the sort of service we can provide."

This morning I was helping a kid who had problems with a bully. This bigger kid was asking for money, and getting it, from this kid every day. We worked that out.
—**Teen Volunteer Abbie Allanach,
Natural Peer Helpers, Southbury, Connecticut**

This kind of peer helping, known usually as "peer mediation", has become rather common in middle schools and high schools, usually as a service of the school guidance department. It goes by various names, from just plain Peer Helpers to Natural Peer Helpers to, in at least one school, PHASE, Peers Helping All Students Equally.

If you join Natural Peer Helpers, you will get involved not only in solving problems but in raising money. A typical high school chapter must come up with about $1,000 every year to cover the cost of training sessions, since the organization is not usually supported by the school budget. So you get a chance to practice your fund-raising skills as well as your counseling skills.

Another way you can put your volunteer energy to work in peer counseling is through the kind of activity that was set up by a director of Youth and Family Services in a Connecticut town. She and several other youth service directors applied for a grant to fund them while they explored ways to blunt the spread of the AIDS virus in the teen population. "Our goal was to look at the effectiveness of kids reaching other kids," says Sharon Lawler-Guck, the director. "We wanted to look at how effective our kids are at coming up with their own ideas, bringing the information to kids in a way that's meaningful throughout the community."

In this kind of work, using grant money, you get to plan, develop, and measure the outcome of a project that you care about. For example, perhaps you organize focus groups to look at the drug and alcohol situation in your school and town. You bring in other kids not only to talk about the problem but to plan services that do something about it.

The teens want to be heard. They want to continue to meet with people, whether it's teachers or service providers or doctors or parents in the community. They really want to be involved.

—Director Sharon Lawler-Guck,
Youth and Family Services, Inc.,
Southbury, Connecticut

Many teens are more comfortable talking with their peers than with adults about many subjects—from AIDS and sex to drugs and alcohol, from boy-girl relations to peer pressure and prejudice. Peer counseling is a service that teens increasingly provide for each other. If you're good at it, your peers can benefit immeasurably.

LITERACY VERSUS ILLITERACY

Two national organizations provide volunteer tutors who can teach reading, writing, and speaking skills to people who are functionally illiterate or who may be literate in another language but cannot read, write or speak English. They are Laubach Literacy Action and Literacy Volunteers of America (LVA). Laubach provides some 900 literacy programs nationwide. LVA delivers tutoring services through a network of more than 50,000 volunteers across the country.

(Courtesy: Patricia Heck/Club RIF, Red Mountain High School, Mesa, AZ)

National organizations provide literacy volunteers on a local basis. At Red Mountain High School in Mesa, Arizona, this teenage girl participates in Club RIF and is among 1,300 members who teach younger children better reading skills.

If you volunteer with either one, what will you be doing? You may be tutoring basic reading skills. Or you may be teaching English as a Second Language. In either case, you are likely to be working with peers or with people younger than you, simply because the experts have found that many adults who need help feel awkward about being taught by teens. There are, however, significant exceptions to this rule. Generally speaking, Laubach teen volunteers seem to get more chances to work with adults than do LVA volunteers.

Suppose you have taken the basic reading course provided by LVA. During a free period, you meet one-on-one in the school library with ninth- or tenth-grade students. Their teachers have picked them out because their reading levels are significantly lower than they should be and they just cannot get their work done. In a typical exercise, the teacher asks you to work with newspapers. You have the students find stories that capture their interest, through a headline or a picture. You have them write about what the story tells them and what they feel about it.

FRONT-PAGE NEWS

"The students pick which story they're the most comfortable with," says Rebecca Blonski, a teen volunteer with Literacy Volunteers of America–Danbury, Inc., in Connecticut. "I've noticed that most of the time it comes from the front page, because that's where they are centered. They won't go through the pages.

"But sometimes I get people into the local section, and into the section where the kids' column is. But mostly it's from the front page—something from a court case or a recent murder that they are interested in."

While you're teaching literacy, you may also be teaching citizenship. And that means teaching adults who are immigrants. Jeorgette Knoll is an administrator for Laubach Literacy Action in Coon Rapids, Minnesota. She helped set up the Communications Academy inside the Coon Rapids High School. "The academy is made up of a core group of kids," she explains, "whose long-term goals are in the communications field. So their experience is in communications classes and skills while they are in high school. They planned, marketed and

(Courtesy: Jeorgette Knoll, Metro North Volunteer Center, Coon Rapids, MN)

The students pictured here are from the Communications Academy at Coon Rapids High School in Minnesota, and they tutored the citizenship classes for the Metro North Adult Basic Education program.

implemented a citizenship class for adults. First, they volunteered to develop the curriculum, and then they taught the class.

"It led to citizenship for several people, and then to more groups studying English as a Second Language. The project was several months long, and we were extremely pleased with the outcome. There were about 40 kids involved, of whom probably 20 or more were actually tutoring. And then in our regular English as a Second Language program, we often have high-school students who go through the training and tutor adults."

As this indicates, teens can and do teach English as a Second Language to adults. Hilary Major of Coon Rapids describes what she did as a Laubach teen volunteer teaching adults:

"I taught English grammar for three seasons. The first season, I worked from a waste management book. The other two seasons, I gave out worksheets on grammar—pronouns, vocabulary, positioning words. I spent a lot of time going over tenses—past, present, future. I tried to make the learning positive, getting my students involved in dialogue. I'd hand out a worksheet, go over it, and make them read sentences and go over the writing exercises. I'd often help with spelling and handwriting. In vocabulary, sometimes they'd just have the right word but the wrong tense.

"And then I'd have my students put their sentences on the board and we'd all go over them after class to see how they did, how they phrased it, alternative ways of saying the same thing in English, sometimes mistakes. Sometimes I corrected handwriting or mistakes in spelling that they'd done.

"Sometimes I'd also go over slang, and 'Whaddayou want?' and 'Whatcha doin?' Instead of classic English, I'd make them write what they'd actually hear.

"I really tried to get them talking to each other, because I had students from Russia, Bosnia, Korea, Mexico, Vietnam, and Guatemala. The only language they could talk to each other in was English. It was really kind of cool. You get people from all over the world—refugees, wanderers—and they're all talking and complaining, in English, about raising their children. I felt like I was part of the United Nations."

TEACHING ENGLISH TO NON-ENGLISH-SPEAKING STUDENTS

Daniel Osnoss, a teen volunteer with Literacy Volunteers of America–Danbury, Inc., in Connecticut, took the LVA's 18-hour training course. "Basically," he says, "it taught me teaching techniques using English instead of a person's native language. I would introduce a few vocabulary words in every lesson. Those included mostly survival skills, because that's what you want to teach so they can get around on their own.

"You use a lot of visual learning, because you're not really supposed to use their native language. So if the word was "ruler", you'd have to show a ruler and show how you use it instead of just saying the Spanish word for a ruler. Or you'd say. 'I am walking.' And you'd actually walk and show the person so they visualize it and actually see what they're learning. That's basically the main technique. But I've had students at different levels, and each required different skills. With the highest level, I got to teach more of the verb conjugations and grammar, as opposed to the lower levels, which calls for more of really the survival vocabulary and how to get your ideas across."

In short, you do not have to know a foreign language in order to teach English as a Second Language. And you can tailor your tutoring to very specific targets. "We try to help learners focus on tangible goals," says Elizabeth Baker, case manager with Literacy Volunteers of America–Southeastern Fairfield County, Inc., in Connecticut. "We ask the learners to tell us what they want to learn."

This means, for example, that a mother may want to learn enough English to converse with her child's teacher or to deal with the process of attaining citizenship, as well as the more commonplace need to

(Continued on page 42)

(Continued from page 41)

cope with a trip to the grocery store. "And the tutors," says Baker, "are delighted to have something to focus on."

If you have studied a foreign language in high school, you know it is a lot more difficult to learn than your native English, which you speak without giving it a thought. Recent research explains why, and gives you an understanding of the challenge you face in tutoring a peer or an adult in English as a Second Language. The research was reported in *The New York Times:*

> As thousands of teen-agers who have struggled to engrave high school French on recalcitrant neurons might have guessed, a new study has found that second languages are stored differently in the human brain depending on when they are learned.
>
> Babies who learn two languages simultaneously, and apparently effortlessly, have a single brain region for generating complex speech, researchers say. But people who learn a second language in adolescence or adulthood possess two such brain regions, one for each language.

What the researchers found was that how your brain handles learning a language depends on your age. A baby uses hearing, vision, touch and movement in learning to talk, and it processes the information from all its senses into a single region of its brain. "Once cells in this region become tuned to one or more languages," reported the *Times,* "they become fixed. If two languages are acquired at this time, they become intermingled. But people who learn a second language in high school [or in adulthood] have to acquire new skills for generating the complex speech sounds of the new tongue, which may explain why a second language is harder to learn."[1] In effect, a second region of the brain is called on to handle the second language.

---

[1] "When an Adult Adds a Language, It's One Brain, Two Systems." *The New York Times,* Tuesday, July 15, 1997, page C4.

(Courtesy: Lee Kozlowski/Literacy Volunteers–Valley Shore, Westbrook, CT)

The headquarters for the Literacy Volunteers of America–Valley Shore is located in Westbrook, Connecticut. Part of a volunteer's job is meeting regularly with coworkers to discuss the curriculum.

High school senior Stacey Robida studied tutoring with Literacy Volunteers of America–Valley Shore, Connecticut. She taught English as a Second Language to a brother and sister from Haiti who spoke only French. She tutored them for an hour and a half a day, three days a week.

"I took French for four years in high school," says Stacey, "so I was able to talk with them when no one else could. We started with a picture dictionary. We went over basic words, stuff you use in everyday life to go to the grocery store or whatever. I'd say the words in English and French and we'd have the picture.

"They were two smart children. The sixth-grader has just finished reading his first novel, *The Call of the Wild,* by Jack London. He read it all by himself. He'd read a chapter a day and explain to me what had happened—in his own words—so I could tell he was understanding it. The little girl and I would play word games like Scrabble."

SUPPORT SERVICES, TOO

Besides tutoring, you can help fight illiteracy by giving your time in the local offices of the literacy organizations. An LVA office, for example, can keep you busy handling phone calls, filing, copying, and performing other clerical work.

CHAPTER THREE
What It Takes to Work in Education and Literacy

Working to help educate others will provide you with challenging and rewarding experiences. As a teen volunteer, there are several items that will be required of you. These include:
- strength and stamina
- commitment
- basic skills and basic training
- good attitude and aptitude, and
- good grades.

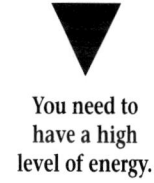

You need to have a high level of energy.

STRENGTH AND STAMINA
What it takes to tutor your peers, little kids or adults is, first, good physical condition. You need to have a high level of energy. Even for an inexhaustible teenager, an hour and a half of concentration on helping someone learn can be very tiring.

How old do you have to be? That depends. Junior volunteers in many libraries start as young as nine. But for most volunteer opportunities in education and literacy you are expected to be at least a ninth-grader—age 14 or so.

COMMITMENT

As in any work you volunteer for, the professionals you work with will expect dependability more than anything else. They don't want to waste time training you if they cannot rely on you to be there when you say you'll be there and do what you say you'll do.

What makes you dependable is your own interest in the work. Do you have a strong interest in reading? Are you thinking of becoming a teacher? A librarian? Does the whole field of education and learning appeal to you? Your interest in such areas will dictate your commitment to helping others improve their learning skills or get a handle on this language you already know so well.

Usually, a tutor in Literacy Volunteers of America (LVA) is asked to commit to at least two hours of tutoring each week for one year. "It's very hard to get people to clear that much time," says Elizabeth Baker, case manager in English as a Second Language with Literacy Volunteers of America–Southeastern Fairfield County, Inc., in Connecticut. "It is a lot. We ask more of our volunteers than other organizations because our volunteers do the core work."

In a typical assignment, if you are tutoring English as a Second Language, LVA gives you two to four students to work with. "This gives the learners more opportunity to use their English," says Baker.

They need tutors who will always show up, because the kids start to depend on them. So you need to be dedicated and take responsibility.

—Teen Tutor Melva Jones,
Children's Community School,
Waterbury, Connecticut

In Club RIF (Reading Is Fundamental), for example, what it takes to be a member is very simple. As teen tutor Brandy Grant of Mesa, Arizona, puts it, "Anybody can join Club RIF. You just have to have a love for books, a love for children, and want to be active." She says Club RIF's annual all-school assembly gets hundreds of members involved. "Through the assembly," she says, "everybody knows what kind of club we are and what we represent."

We can tell the teenagers' interest just by their interaction with the children and their inquisitiveness and whether they show they want to learn.
—Director Muriel Moore,
Head Start, Waterbury, Connecticut

BASIC SKILLS AND BASIC TRAINING

Volunteering to help expand education and literacy requires some basic training and basic skills. The skills and training you need depend on the setting in which you choose to work.

In the Library

Suppose you volunteer in a public library. You need bring no particular skills other than your interest. "Every child who applies to volunteer," says Leslie Barban, children's room manager at the Richland County Public Library in Columbia, South Carolina, "is interviewed, trained and treated as a valued member of the team."

Training in a typical library includes an orientation session that tells you what your work will include. You may learn how to fill in a time card. You'll find out why wearing a name tag is important. You'll discover the value of working independently without being supervised by library staffers. You may do some role playing—where you interrupt a staff person who is helping someone on the phone or in person, or you pretend to have trouble dealing with a request for a book or videotape, or you play the game the kids will be playing in the summer reading club.

The purpose of all this is to put you at ease with the library's rules and habits. It also teaches you how to deal with the varying age levels of the library's patrons so you can be depended on to handle most situations without supervision.

LEARNING AT THE LIBRARY

"We have orientation meetings where we show the teen volunteers what the reading club consists of," says Amy Pittman, young adult librarian at the Danbury (Connecticut) Public Library.

"But the teenagers learn it right with the kids," notes Pittman. "They also learn how to interact with people, and to be responsible—things that people don't really think of as skills. They do learn a lot. By the end, they're really, really good at it. And I have lots and lots of repeaters. They come back year after year."

TUTORING YOUR PEERS—OR YOUNGER KIDS

Suppose you feel you can help other students your age, or maybe only a grade or two below you. Georgia Ann Hayes, a guidance counselor at Meekins Middle School in Stuttgart, Arkansas, describes the three required criteria to be a peer tutor in her school's program:

> The students must attend a workshop, which makes them aware of the need for reading. They also are made aware of the need for being careful about the feelings of others. It's a relationship thing as well.
>
> Once they've done that, they are assigned to students.

I look at those who are not doing well, and I ask them if they're interested in having someone assist them. I assign a peer tutor at the same grade level, and hopefully in the same classes. That way the peer tutor knows what work the other person is being assigned. And I do a check sheet of things they're expected to do.

What qualifies someone to be a peer tutor? We have three criteria. First I look at their achievement test scores. But I do not require anything more than just average, because sometimes an average person can offer more assistance than someone who is really bright. And so I usually say, 50th percentile or better on their achievement test composite score.

Then I look at grades. Usually I'll allow one C, but I want mostly As and Bs. Otherwise the tutors are not going to be able to help someone else—they need to work on their own grades.

Lastly, I send my list around for teacher recommendations. That doesn't mean the teachers have to recommend them. It means they say yes or no. And unless this peer tutor is a big discipline problem, the answer is always yes.

The three criteria are very easy to meet. But first and foremost, the peer tutor has to have the desire to help someone else. So they have to request it themselves.

How about tutoring younger kids, even as young as Head Start preschoolers? What training do you need? None, says Ellen Block, coordinator of volunteers at Lenox Hill Neighborhood House in New York City. "You don't need any particular skills to do this," she says, "just basic intelligence. The teens don't get training, except perhaps on the job in terms of learning to sit more quietly or read more slowly. But there's no training in the strict sense."

◀ EXPANDING EDUCATION & LITERACY: OPPORTUNITIES TO VOLUNTEER ▶

(Courtesy: Patricia Heck/Club RIF, Red Mountain High School, Mesa, AZ)

Club RIF member Kerry Siep visits a homeless shelter in Mesa, Arizona, for a book distribution event.

You have to have a lot of patience, especially with the little kids. It's kind of hard to get them interested right away. But once you get them interested, you're all right. You just have to have a little patience.
—Teen Tutor Dustan Flahart, Club RIF,
Red Mountain High School, Mesa, Arizona

Nor is there strict training in Club RIF. "Really, all you have to do is be willing and like kids," says Meaghan Kennedy, teen volunteer in Club RIF at Red Mountain High School in Mesa, Arizona. "You can just enroll in the class. Once you're in it, you get all the training you need. We have a program called Q.R.Q.—Question, Read, Question. It's a way to teach people how to read to little kids. You read the title of the book, ask them a question that associates with the book, and you read them some of the story and ask questions while you read to get them involved. The Q.R.Q. is the main thing, that's what we concentrate on, spending time with the kids and interacting with them. We have kind of an interesting exercise, once we've gone through Q.R.Q. Everyone in the class at the high school has to sit in the audience and act like second-graders. A person who just went through Q.R.Q. reads the story and we try and act like the second-graders would and give the person an idea of what it's going to be like. It's role playing. That's always fun."

Peer Counseling

Working with a group like Natural Peer Helpers, on the other hand, calls for some very specific preparation. Typically, you spend three intensive days—a Friday, say, then the next Monday and the following Friday—training for the program. You might even be excused from school classes, so you can put in full days.

Abbie Allanach, a highschool senior who is an experienced Natural Peer Helper, describes the training.

> It's a process by which the group learns to communicate with each other. By sharing our own experiences with helping others, with helping ourselves and through learning about each other, we learn about people in general.
>
> We learn how to form a listening relationship, how to form a peer helping relationship with someone, which is very different from a counseling relationship or just a friendship. We learn about crisis situations. We learn to gauge how explosive a situation is. We learn how to determine whether we need to get help for this person immediately or whether it is a situation where danger may not be approaching for several days or weeks.
>
> We also learn to deal with such questions as, "To what extent can I help this person?" and, "When do I have to turn over the situation to a professional?"
>
> How do people get into being Peer Helpers? The way that other people joined the group is they came to the meetings. You see, at the beginning of each year, we start off with a couple of weeks of just introductory meetings. We meet once a week for an hour to two hours. We start off by explaining what Peer Helpers is about, so if you're there you know the sort of commitment that you're getting yourself into. People who go to the meetings to start with already have an inclination toward it. They feel that Peer Helpers is something they'd like to join. They already know that much about themselves. Then after going to a couple of meetings, people pretty much know whether or not it's for them. At the beginning of the year, after there've only been a couple of meetings, four people kind

of disappeared who we figured would never really buy into this. The people who stayed on board are the ones who are dedicated. They're the ones who know what kind of good the group can do. It has to be a commitment on their part, to come every week, to make sure they keep in touch. You find out very quickly whether or not people will want to do this just by whether or not they stay on, whether or not they stay committed to the group.

Teaching Literacy

Whether you volunteer with Laubach Literacy Action or with Literacy Volunteers of America (LVA), you will go through a training period. Laubach, as mentioned earlier, works more with teens than does LVA. At Laubach, you have a better chance of teaching illiterate adults of all ages—Americans who are functionally illiterate or immigrants who want to learn English as a Second Language. At LVA, you are more likely to be teaching English as a Second Language to your peers or to students younger than you. Laubach also concentrates on creating and publishing materials for the instruction of your students, while LVA creates materials for training the teacher.

In your training at LVA, you report to their headquarters or to a library for three training sessions a week, each about two hours long, for two or three weeks. You work in a group, doing role playing and practicing on tutoring each other.

To start out at Literacy Volunteers, I had to take an 18-hour training course. It taught me certain techniques for teaching English, such as using English instead of the person's native language.

—**Teen Tutor Daniel Osnoss,
Literacy Volunteers of America–Danbury, Inc.,**

Hilary Major, a teenage tutor of Spanish-speaking adults, describes the training she received at the Metro North Adult Basic Education Volunteer Center in Coon Rapids, Minnesota, to teach English as a Second Language in the Laubach Literacy program.

> As a student teacher, I observed classrooms and I did lessons. I hung out with the students and talked with them and listened to them. I learned to listen really well, because I had to sort through half a dozen different accents and various levels of fluency. And I learned to hear how the Indonesian people, for instance, pronounce English versus how European people pronounce English.
>
> One of the things I showed them was how to physically move their mouths so their tongues can make certain sounds. The "th," for instance, is a considerably hard sound to make. In any language but English, the "th" sound isn't there. And there was a checklist of stuff I had to go over and fill out.
>
> I had to learn how to use a variety of computer programs, one of which was called Rosetta Stone—which was not so great for the higher-level students, but for the lower-level ones it was really good because it showed the word, the action, and it vocalized the sentence and vocabulary. So that was really quite useful, and they liked that.

Your training may include some techniques that are surprising. In the Laubach program in Minneapolis, Michael Weinbeck learned how to use closed-caption television as a classroom tool in teaching English as a Second Language. The superimposed captions, provided for deaf people to read, enabled students to read the English words they were hearing on the sound tracks. Michael found this to be an ideal learning situation.

Your training may even include a musical approach. Michael learned that some of the rhythms used in jazz could be used with everyday sentences. "We had a program using music and metrically based sentences," he says. "It imparted in the student a sense of timing in the speech. The tutor would say the sentences and the students repeated after them. Some tutors really got into it and they would clap their hands and go back and forth."

GOOD ATTITUDE AND APTITUDE

Probably the most important asset you can bring to tutoring is "people skills"—the ability to get along with others, to listen, to put your ideas across in a friendly, positive way. You cannot be shy.

If your students are younger, you have to be careful not to talk down to them. You must not seem to be superior or arrogant—even if you do actually know more. Even with little kids in Head Start, or in first or second grade, you have to be sensitive to the fact that their minds are just as sharp and inquisitive as yours. You are there to help them make the best use of their minds—not to pound lessons into their heads like nails into a board.

▼
Their minds are just as sharp and inquisitive as yours.

I think the most important thing with little children is patience. You have to try to understand them and get them to work. It can be quite difficult because you have to speak to them so that they understand.

*—Tutor Sara Copetto,
Children's Community School,
Waterbury, Connecticut*

If you get an opportunity to tutor adults, it gives you a chance to show your own maturity—in two ways. First, you show that you can stick to it. One reason the LVA is reluctant to use teens is its concern that teenagers' school schedules shift and their interests change. George Demetrion, an executive at LVA, notes, "Continuity in the tutoring is really critical if you're going to be effective. You need to see that the tutor is going to be really reliable—that's one of the bottom lines."

The second way is also a question of attitude. Demetrion describes this concern.

> If you're a teenager working with adults aged anywhere from the 20s to the 70s, you have to consider the issue of equity. When you link a 16-year-old with a 63-year-old grandmother who maybe can't read but who knows one heck of a lot about the world—much more than the teen—that doesn't mean there can't be relationships. But the teenager has to have some understanding of the depth of life experience. That's very critical. I think the key is when the teenagers are supported within their own high school programs, and it is part of their curriculum. Then it makes sense to have teenagers support the tutoring or provide some of the tutoring.

As a tutor, you have to be persistent. "You just keep trying, and don't give up," says Stacey Robida, a high school senior who tutors younger children in English as a Second Language through Literacy Volunteers of America–Valley Shore, Connecticut. "If you give up on them, they're going to see that. Sometimes, you think, 'How am I going to explain this to them?' A lot of times, acting it out or showing them pictures or just showing a different way really helps them."

GOOD GRADES IN SCHOOL

If you want to be a tutor or peer helper, must you maintain a certain grade average? No. There are a few requirements in some cases, but they seem to be quite flexible.

Club RIF welcomes every student who wants to join, regardless of the marks he or she is getting in any courses. Many high school chapters of the National Honor Society invite their members to volunteer as tutors. That's how Steve Brady got involved in tutoring at the Children's Community School in Waterbury, Connecticut. But Melva Jones, who also tutors there, is not a member of the National Honor Society. She simply heard that the school needed tutors and asked for an interview.

On the other hand, some National Honor Society chapters have formal arrangements with LVA. Society members take the LVA's training course each year and are then offered tutoring assignments.

▼

Club RIF welcomes every student who wants to join.

My training is good forever. If I don't have time for Literacy Volunteers when I'm in college, I can go into it when I'm an adult.

**—Teen Tutor Kristi Auer,
Literacy Volunteers of America–Danbury, Inc.,
Connecticut**

CHAPTER FOUR

What's in It for You?

One question everybody asks about volunteering is, "What's in it for me?" There are a number of answers to that question.

CAREER BENEFITS

If you're thinking about a future in education or library work, this kind of volunteering is a natural. Tutoring your peers or older or younger people can give you good insight into what teaching involves—the discipline and patience you need, the self-reliance it demands, the rewarding feeling of achievement you get when you know you have succeeded in teaching something to another person.

Most Club RIF volunteers think about teaching kids because it's so much fun. You think, "Gosh, I could really do this every day. I could go to a school and I could be a teacher." It definitely influences you.
—Teen Volunteer Brandy Grant,
Club RIF, Red Mountain High School,
Mesa, Arizona

Head Start Director Muriel Moore of Waterbury, Connecticut, says, "Some teens who volunteer to teach preschool kids see it as a career goal. Some are expecting to be teachers. Often members of the high school Future Teachers Club participate. Some do it as an exploratory

(V. Harlow/Community Action for Greater Middletown, Middletown CT)

Tiffany McNeil enjoys reading to two little girls at the Head Start program in Middletown, Connecticut. Tiffany, a student at the Woodrow Wilson Middle School, is able to volunteer through an alternative program her school sponsors.

measure. They want to see what it is like to work with young children. They go into Head Start one semester and volunteer in the health field or something else in another."

Teens agree that volunteering in the field of education and literacy looks good on a college application and on a résumé. "It's a really big deal for colleges," says Danielle Storhoff, who tutored English as a Second Language for Literacy Volunteers of America–Danbury, Inc., in Connecticut, during her first two years in high school. "I hadn't really thought about it, but I was talking with one person who's going to college and she was telling me about how valuable community service is. And then our director was telling me how Literacy Volunteers is a big part of community service. I'm really glad I did LVA because it will help me later on."

I applied to my college in August, and they asked for my transcripts and everything. Well, I had just sent them my transcripts, but I hadn't sent them my essay yet. And five days after I sent my transcripts, they accepted me, just on the basis of my academic record and my community service as a literacy volunteer. I really think it did help.
—Teen Volunteer Stacey Robida,
Literacy Volunteers of America–Valley Shore,
Westbrook, Connecticut

Danbury High School junior Rebecca Blonski, who tutored her peers in ninth and tenth grades through LVA, is thinking of a career in education, specializing in working with the deaf. "People have always told me that it's great that I'm tutoring in literacy because colleges look for experience like this," she says. "But I don't do it for that. I do it because I like to work with people. And because helping me relate to students is good. Next year, because I'm in peer leadership in the National Honor Society, they'll be looking for a lot of community service, and this will count. And a lot of people I know are all of a sudden going to be in it because of that. But I've been in it for a while. I just wanted to see what it was like for myself."

SELF-DISCIPLINE

Volunteering to work in the fields of education and literacy provides you with practice in self-discipline. When you tutor someone, you find out how important it is to be patient. You have to understand, for instance, that pride is a factor in learning. No one likes to lose face or be put down. So your students may not admit that they don't "get it" during a tutoring session. When you realize that maybe you are going over their heads, you have to find the patience to take a simpler approach. You have to find their level without seeming to be superior to them.

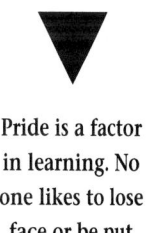

Pride is a factor in learning. No one likes to lose face or be put down.

Many students don't want to look bad. Sometimes they may not understand a word but they tell you they do. They just don't want to go through the emotional thing of admitting that they don't understand.

—Teen Tutor Rebecca Blonski,
Literacy Volunteers of America–Danbury, Inc.,
Connecticut

Tutoring also gives you good practice in budgeting your time. Usually you will have specific assignments from the teachers, if you are helping younger kids with reading, math, history or science. If you are teaching English as a Second Language, you will have lesson plans that come out of your training. You will face specific time limits—class periods during school hours, perhaps an hour and a half maximum after school in the afternoon. And if a scheduling conflict makes you miss a session, you'll have to find the time to make it up.

All this balances against your time for your own homework, household chores, sports and recreation, and maybe a part-time paid job. And don't forget your social life. You soon get into the discipline of working out schedules and knowing when you must be where.

> ### A LESSON IN BUDGETING TIME
>
> "I did the reading lessons only on weekends and a little on Monday nights," says Stacey Robida, a teen volunteer with Literacy Volunteers of America–Valley Shore, Connecticut. "And I was also editor of my high school yearbook, so it was all a matter of budgeting my time.
>
> "There were a few times when I had to tell the kids I wouldn't be there for the next session because of other school commitments. They understood. And I made it up to them on a different day."

INCREASING YOUR OWN KNOWLEDGE

Helping others learn helps you in terms of your own education and understanding of the world. Meaghan Kennedy describes what she got out of working in Club RIF in Mesa, Arizona.

> Above all, I gained a definite love of community service. A lot of kids think community service is kind of hard to get involved in, but this club is all about community service. I have never experienced such a wonderful relationship with kids. By reading with them I became aware of how important reading really is. I also learned how important it is to read to children and to spend time with them.
>
> And it has made me think about teaching. What I'd really love to do, though, is write. So it's made me think about writing children's stories, or writing a curriculum

based on them. So I think that's what I'll really take away, as well as just really fun memories of spending time with everybody.

Hilary Major, a teen volunteer in the Laubach Literacy Action program, spoke just after completing her senior year in high school. She had taught English as a Second Language through the Metro North Adult Basic Education Volunteer Center in Coon Rapids, Minnesota.

>It was really great for me because I was learning something about the problems in America and I was doing it by helping someone learn English, so they could help themselves in their own lives.
>
>One woman from Bosnia started the first season I did. She graduated the last season I did. The first day I walked in to see what was going on was the day she came in to test. She had no comprehension. By the third season, she was fluent and holding conversations in English. She also planned to go to a community college to get a degree. That had a big impact on me.
>
>That type of stuff, where I was able to help them help themselves, was really valuable for me. I kind of went into it thinking, O.K., I'll try this out and see what happens, and I stuck with it a lot longer than I thought I would.
>
>I met people from Africa and India as well. I saw how valuable I was to them as an American who would sit and talk with them for five minutes about the weather, about the children, and then just do some little practices. I realized how important it was for me to be patient enough to listen to them stumble through English. It made my own country and my own language more valuable to me.
>
>And at the same time, the Vietnam War means more to me now because I know one of the families who fought in

it. My best friend is a Vietnamese immigrant. She's quite fluent in English, but her parents aren't. Some things she's said catch me quite by surprise. 'Cross my liver and hope to live,' instead of 'Cross my heart and hope to die.' It's really made my own country and my own language more valuable to me.

Bosnia means more to me because I've worked with people who have left there. I've talked to people for whom these countries were their home. That was their home, not just an article in a newspaper. I feel a lot more conscious of that, and it's meant a lot more to me.

Such a knowledge of other people, and such a respect for them, can be one of the most valuable things you get out of volunteering in a tutoring program.

OTHER SKILLS

You also gain some practical skills. You can learn about organizing your peers and younger students when you help run a schoolwide Club RIF program or set up seminars on leadership through Chain Reaction. You find out how meetings can be kept orderly through *Robert's Rules of Order.* You practice communication skills in writing notices for bulletin boards and announcements for the public-address system, as well as newsletters and reports.

Fund-raising is an important skill you can gain in this type of volunteer work. Not just car washes, but the do's and don'ts of writing letters and making telephone calls to ask for money. Even more complex is the challenge of getting grant money, which requires becoming familiar with grant application forms. If you are involved, you will become familiar with such forms. You will find out why you need to include detailed backup material to support your application. You will make presentations and await decisions.

(Courtesy: Danielle Storhoff)

Danielle Storhoff is a member of Literacy Volunteers of America and lives in Danbury, Connecticut. Danielle has taught English as a Second Language for this group over the past two years.

GETTING MONEY IS DIFFICULT

"We're making a presentation to the Parent-Teacher Organization," says Abbie Allanach, teen volunteer with Natural Peer Helpers in Southbury, Connecticut, "because we want to try to win a grant from them, to help pay for our training sessions. But getting money from the school is very, very difficult. So we're keeping a log for a month, to show just how often we meet with people and what problems we meet with them for. We just started the log a week ago, and we already have 10 counseling sessions in it. And that's with only seven Peer Helpers working."

SATISFACTION

Maybe the simplest and best answer to "What's in it for me?" lies in the word *satisfaction*. Georgia Ann Hayes, a guidance counselor at the Meekins Middle School in Stuttgart, Arkansas, lines up students to work with Laubach Literacy Action. "What's in it for the peer tutor," she says, "is satisfaction. Other than that, a half-day workshop, usually with pizza served—and the kids don't even know about that ahead of time. We have check sheets that ask, 'Why do you want to be here?' And we discuss this, and they just say, 'I want to be able to help someone else.' Ninety percent of the time, that's the answer I get."

I was the youngest person in the classroom. I loved working with the adults. Sometimes I told them that I was not being paid to do this, and the look on their faces was great.

—**Laubach Literacy Action Teen Volunteer Hilary Major,
Metro North Adult Basic Education
Volunteer Center,
Coon Rapids, Minnesota**

Tutoring English as a Second Language, Daniel Osnoss, who works with Literacy Volunteers of America–Danbury, Inc., in Connecticut, has reached the same conclusion. "It's nice to see someone who comes from somewhere else and really wants to assimilate," he says. "It's nice to see his or her progression throughout the year. There's real satisfaction in seeing that person get along and be able to take care of himself or herself."

Kristi Auer, another teen in the Danbury LVA group, agrees. "I just love helping people, and that's a big thing for me," says Kristi. "I mean, to see the looks on their faces when they finally figure out that they are able to read and understand without you having to put in a little bit of help or go back over something."

Sometimes you almost don't realize that what you are doing is successful. After two years of tutoring English as a Second Language for Literacy Volunteers of America–Danbury, Inc., in ninth and tenth grade, Danielle Storhoff said, "As far as satisfaction, I just like the fact that I'm helping someone who needs help. Sometimes I don't think I'm helping at all. But I was in English class and this woman came up to me and said, 'I'm Sandra's English teacher. She'd been failing my class and then you started working with her. Now she's pulling a B-plus.' So I was excited to hear this had happened, because it gave me the feeling that I had helped her."

You can find two kinds of satisfaction, according to Kristen Moore, a teen volunteer in charge of special projects in the South Dakota chapter of the March of Dimes Chain Reaction Youth Leadership Council in Sioux Falls. One, she says, is "the overwhelming feeling that you've done something to help other students realize that they can get something out of volunteering. A lot of kids think, 'Why should I waste my time volunteering?' But when they come to our events and see how much fun it actually can be, it gets them going."

The other satisfaction involves changing people's attitudes. "In our community," says Kristen, "sometimes the youth get a bad rap. It's kind of an older community, and when they think of youth they think of the negative side of it. We're trying to prove them wrong and prove that we do make a difference. Through the media, and lots of places, many people in the community are now realizing that."

The satisfaction? Knowing that I'm giving someone the opportunity to gain knowledge.
—Tutor Steve Brady,
Children's Community Center,
Waterbury, Connecticut

Asked about the satisfactions he found in tutoring, Michael Weinbeck, who worked with Laubach Literacy International in Minneapolis, said, "Initially, I wanted to teach literacy to adults. The Laubach administrator sort of discouraged that because I was so young. I was 17 at the time when I was getting involved in the program and she said there were problems teaching someone several decades older than I how to read. So she suggested the English as a Second Language program, where I could teach adults. So I approached it with a different goal in mind.

"As far as what I derived from the whole experience, I got my greatest satisfactions when I saw people really picking up skills that I was trying to teach them—and when I felt they were comfortable with me as a teacher. Obviously, most of them were much older than I, so at times there was a bit of discomfort in connection with that, but at other times I really felt like things were clicking and people were really comfortable with me as a teacher and that I was doing a good job. That was the satisfaction that kept me coming back every week."

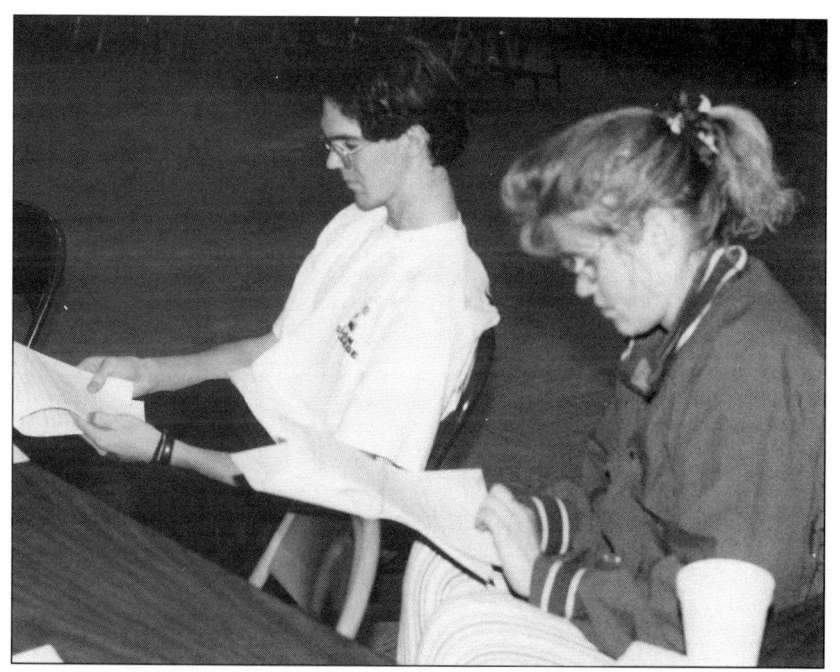

(Courtesy: Frank Young/March of Dimes Birth Defects Foundation)

Nathan Byerly, teen chairperson with the Chain Reaction Leadership Council in Winston-Salem, North Carolina, attends one of his group meetings.

GIVING BACK

"I enjoy volunteering," says Nathan Byerly, teen chairperson with the Chain Reaction Leadership Council in Winston-Salem, North Carolina. "I'm the kind of person who likes to give back to the community. I just enjoy doing it—actually making a difference of some kind."

Nathan's group puts on several fund-raisers and conferences each year. Perhaps the most important are leadership-building conferences for high school students. The group also makes presentations at

(Continued on page 70)

(Continued from page 69)

school meetings to support an October competition among schools to see which can raise the largest amount within a week for the annual Dime Drive. They sponsor TeamWalk, which supports the March of Dimes' WalkAmerica. They participate as volunteers in their chapter's annual event called the North Carolina Chili Championship and Rubber Duck Regatta. Their annual health conference in February brings medical experts from local hospitals to the high schools to speak on such health issues as teen pregnancy, AIDS and nutrition. Altogether, says Nathan, "it has helped me a lot to realize that in the future I want to be involved in volunteer activities."

CHAPTER FIVE
Is It Right for You?

The way to answer this question—is it *right* for you?—is to look at the advantages and satisfactions that you can get from tutoring or counseling people, as well as the disadvantages and dissatisfactions you may have to face. When you have reviewed some of these, give yourself the quiz, provided at the end of this chapter, to determine if this area is right for you.

You improve your own self-image or self-esteem.

ADVANTAGES AND SATISFACTIONS

Working with people in the teaching and counseling professions helps you find out whether you want to concentrate on these fields when you get to college and later in your lifework. If you are considering but are not sure about being a teacher, librarian, social worker or psychologist, for example, you can try it out before you make a commitment in terms of your education. Finding out if you like it can save you both time and money in the future.

Let's look at some of the advantages and satisfactions you experience.

Handling Responsibility

In most of the situations described in this book, you get good practice in taking on responsibility. As you succeed in handling it, you gain a second advantage: You improve your self-image or self-esteem. You get to know your own capabilities and limitations.

TEENS TUTORING ADULTS

Jeorgette Knoll, an administrator for the Laubach Literacy Action program in Coon Rapids, Minnesota, describes how teen volunteers handle the responsibility of tutoring adults: "We were real skeptical at first, but we've never had a problem. We had one tutor who started when he was a junior in high school and worked all the way through his third year of college. The adult students were really impressed with him.

"We've had teens team up and teach the adult classes together. They've also taught independently and with other adults. The teenagers do it under the supervision of an on-site instructor, but they are actually teaching the courses. They go through the same training as the adult volunteers, and they have to do the lesson planning like everyone else. It's just been a cooperative thing."

Gaining Recognition

With your voluntary service, you make new friends not only among your peers but also among the adult volunteers and staff with whom you work. Getting their recognition and approval can be especially valuable. For example, they can help you when you need recommendations or references to put on college or job applications.

Making New Friends

Volunteering in a tutoring program, as a Natural Peer Helper, or in a library introduces you to new people beyond your usual group—some your own age, and others who are older or younger than you.

(Courtesy: Jeorgette Knoll, Metro North Volunteer Center, Coon Rapids, MN)

Cooperation is vital, especially when teens learn to tutor adults in a literacy program. Volunteer Nicole Daniels and supervisor Dana Zimmerman were the Vista volunteers who started a cooperative project between Metro North Adult Basic Education and the Coon Rapids High School Communications Academy.

The knowledge that Abbie Allanach has gained as a Natural Peer Helper has given her advantages in personal relationships, she says. Her work at Pomperaug High School in Southbury, Connecticut, gave her "some fundamental knowledge about dealing with other people." While that's essential knowledge for everyone to learn, Abbie feels that Peer Helpers learn it "thankfully, at a very early age. It helps in every relationship. You learn how to come to compromises. You learn how to deal on an equal level with other people."

Brandy Grant, a Club RIF member in Red Mountain High School, Mesa, Arizona, sums up the advantages in a nutshell: "It doesn't really cut into your social life because there are so many members, and a lot of your friends are in it. So you're having fun with your friends. It is a social life itself."

HELPING CHILDREN READ: "IT'S A HERO TYPE OF THING"

"What do the teenagers get out of it?" asks Patricia Heck, a teacher and adviser to Club RIF at Red Mountain High School in Mesa, Arizona. "The young children—the second-graders—absolutely worship and adore them. It's a hero type of thing.

"Very few of the teens were read to when they were children. That's why we developed Reading Buddies—to make sure our volunteers are familiar with children's books and how to read them, and that somebody tells them, 'This is important.' You just assume they know it's important. But they don't. They've got to be told. And they've got to be shown how to do it."

DISADVANTAGES AND DISSATISFACTIONS
Here are the negatives you should think about.

No Pay
You must weigh the advantages you will get from a volunteer job against the disadvantage of giving up time that you could be using to earn money.

Exclusive Commitment
Michael Weinbeck, who tutored adults in English as a Second Language for Laubach Literacy Action during two years in high school, outlines the commitment process: "You did have this commitment once a week. And it was fun. It was a couple of hours where you could not focus on any other issues. When I was there, all I was thinking about was teaching my students. The high school student has a lot of other commitments, and oftentimes it cuts into those things."

Uses Study Periods
Tutoring peers or younger kids in school usually means giving up your own study periods. "That's the time a lot of people spend doing their homework," says Daniel Osnoss, who works with Literacy Volunteers of America–Danbury, Inc. "But if it means doing my homework the night before instead of in school, it's worth spending the time to help another person."

This year I had a really busy schedule and I didn't have lunch. I had one study hall, and that's when I tutored, but I loved tutoring and I looked forward to every Thursday, seventh period, when I tutored. I never felt like, Oh, no, I have to do it again.
—Teen Tutor Kristi Auer,
Literacy Volunteers of America–Danbury, Inc.,
Connecticut

◄ EXPANDING EDUCATION & LITERACY: OPPORTUNITIES TO VOLUNTEER ►

(Courtesy: Patricia Heck/Club RIF, Red Mountain High School, Mesa, AZ)

A love of children and reading is essential if you want to volunteer for Club RIF. The organization regularly holds book distributions like this one for the Gila River Indian Community. Books were handed out to students at St. Peter's Indian School in Mesa, Arizona.

It Takes Time

"The one major problem," says Sara Copetto, teen tutor at the Children's Community School in Waterbury, Connecticut, "is trying to budget your time well enough so you can get all your work done and still be involved in your own school's organizations, like the Peer Helpers. All my work at the Children's School was after school, so I had to miss a couple of meetings for certain organizations. Also it took time, especially during busy periods—like when you have rehearsal for a play or practice for a sport, you're taking away that afternoon. And you're trying to get homework done, so instead the homework's being pushed to 10 o'clock at night."

SELF-QUIZ

Here are some questions to think about:
- Can you commit anywhere from 30 to 200 hours of the school year, or 50 hours of your summer, to this work?
- Can you balance your schoolwork, a paying job and this volunteer job? Not "spread yourself too thin"?
- Can you trust your inner voice, as you ask yourself, "Do I really want to help little kids, my peers or older people?"

A LOVE OF CHILDREN, A LOVE OF READING

"The educational community service comes in with the little kids," says Meaghan Kennedy, a Club RIF member. "You also need a love of reading because you're sharing the immeasurable joys that you can get out of reading to people and reading books on your own. Those are the pluses. Those are what you need to have a passion for."

- Can you work comfortably with an older adult who may speak little or no English at the start of your tutoring sessions?
- Are you willing to "unlearn" some of your own reading habits so you can successfully help first- and second-graders learn to read?

I always thought everybody knew how to read to a child. Well, they don't. I teach high school kids how to read to younger children and give them activities to do. I make sure they're prepared. I haven't had a failure yet.
    —Teacher and Adviser to Club RIF Patricia Heck,
        Red Mountain High School, Mesa, AZ

- Can you speak to a classroom or assembly of schoolmates?
- Are you an organizer? A leader?
- Can you ask questions? When you don't understand, are you willing to say so?
- Do you love reading?
- In such work as peer mentoring, can you maintain your special dedication in the face of frustrations—despite a lack of support, for instance, from others?

DEALING WITH ADULT LEARNERS

"It takes a certain sensibility from the younger tutors to have the maturity to deal with adult learners," says Michael Weinbeck, a Laubach Literacy Action tutor in English as a Second Language in Minneapolis.

"And the tutors must have strong English skills themselves," notes Michael. "You often find that people who have immigrated here from a foreign country—where they were taught a language based on strict grammar rules—want to learn English just by memorizing grammatical rules, which is not usually the best way to learn a language. At the same time, a tutor should know well the grammar of the English language."

(Courtesy: Patricia Heck/Club RIF, Red Mountain High School, Mesa, AZ)

A RIF volunteer enjoys a book with this youngster, who will soon be reading on his own.

Asked what tips she had for future teen tutors, Kristi Auer of Literacy Volunteers of America–Danbury, Inc., in Connecticut, said, "I'd say you have to be patient, because a lot of times you're too eager to help. For example, I'd be helping a student with homework in English as a Second Language. I knew the answer and I wanted to tell him right out, but I knew it's his homework, you know, and he has to do it. So you have to be patient and you have to know how to explain things, but you have to find a different way. A lot of times, they won't understand what you're trying to say the first time, and you have to be creative and find different methods of teaching. I used index cards for words. I used all sorts of things."

MEETING A VOLUNTEER

For an overall picture of what's in it for you, meet Sara Copetto, a freshman at Yale University in New Haven, Connecticut. Sara tutored second-graders at the Children's Community School in Waterbury, Connecticut, every Tuesday and Wednesday afternoon during her junior and senior years in high school. Here is how she responded to questions about the challenges and satisfactions of tutoring little kids.

What's a typical challenge when you're tutoring seven- or eight-year-olds?

The teacher sometimes leaves you a ditto sheet that the kids don't even know. For example, one time this child had a math ditto and she didn't remember ever doing anything like this. So we had to sit down and try and teach her exactly what the whole concept was, because she just didn't understand it. It was the idea of something is greater than or less than something else—say, four is greater than three or less than five. So to sort of help her, because she didn't understand, I went through all kinds of different examples.

Did you have particular techniques for getting them interested?

One student I had didn't know how to tell time, and she just refused to do clocks. She did not like them at all. I figured out that the fact that she didn't know how to tell time meant that she didn't want to do it and embarrass herself. So I drew this big picture of a clock with all the different numbers on it. Beside the one I put the figure five. And beside the two I put a ten. You know, I tried to tear the whole thing apart so she could see how the one could be an hour and also be the five minutes. So I put it both ways. And she liked the fact that I drew her a picture. They love the fact that you can draw them pictures and it'll help them understand it.

How did you get into tutoring the younger kids?

I did it last year just because a boy I knew was a tutor, and he made an announcement in one of our classes that they were low on tutors, and I had never heard of it before then. So I said, O.K., why not, if you need an extra hand, I'll go.

And you discovered you liked it?

Yes, I really enjoy myself with the kids. They really are sweet children. At recess, they'll come over and ask to play with you. Little kids are very appealing. They're always so much fun.

What else do you get out of it?

Well, I decided to come back this year just because it was not only so much fun, it really was educational, because these are what they call high-risk children that we tutor. One of the purposes of the program is to keep them at school instead of sending them home to an empty house, which is what happens in a lot of cases. They want them somewhere with people—you know, to talk to someone.

So it was educational for you?

Yes. When you talk to these children you see how they view certain things. I was talking to one of my students, and her aspiration was to be the manager of McDonald's. Which really surprised me, because I'd been thinking of being a lawyer or a doctor, and she wants to be manager of McDonald's.

And tutoring gave you some perspective?

It sure did. That reminds me of another student. This one asked me who I live with, and I said, "I live with my family." And she said, "Who's that?" Well, you know, that really surprised me, the fact that I needed to define that. It's amazing to see.

That meant you had to explain the concept of a family?

Yes. And it makes you feel good when you finally get a kid to understand a concept. And you get them to think about something. Like when I did the clock thing, I came home and I said, "My student finally did her time today!" That just makes me happy, that moment when they finally get it, when they say, "Oh!"

Has your tutoring influenced your thinking about your future?

Well, I've enjoyed it so much I was thinking of perhaps going into teaching or somehow working with children, because after talking and trying to communicate with the children, which sometimes can be difficult, I've really liked it. It made me happy, asking them questions and answering their questions. So whether I'll be a doctor or a lawyer or a teacher, I don't know at this point.

Chapter Six
Where to Find Opportunities

HOW TO GET MORE INFORMATION

Start your search by checking with English teachers and guidance counselors at your school. Ask if Reading Is Fundamental has set up a Club RIF there. Ask if Literacy Volunteers of America or Laubach Literacy Action is on the scene.

Call or stop in at your public library. They should know about LVA and Laubach and how to get in touch with them. Ask about summer reading clubs and story time for little kids on Saturdays at the library, too.

Put your phone book to work. LVA's local chapters all begin with the words Literacy Volunteers. Laubach's branches may be camouflaged by localized names like Beaver Lake Literacy Council or Central Louisiana Partners in Literacy or Metro North Adult Basic Education. Your library's reference desk can help you find them.

If you're stymied, contact the national organizations:
Reading Is Fundamental, Inc.
600 Maryland Avenue, SW—Suite 600
Smithsonian Institution
Washington, DC 20024
(202) 287-3196

Laubach Literacy Action
1320 Jamesvile Avenue—Box 131
Syracuse, NY 13210
(315) 422-9121

Literacy Volunteers of America, Inc. (LVA)
635 James Street
Syracuse, NY 13203
(315) 472-0001

The National Literacy Hotline, (800) 228-8813, links callers with literacy programs in their areas. And the LVA, which networks 399 community programs in 44 states, maintains the following state offices:

Connecticut	(860) 236-5466
Illinois	(312) 857-1582
Maine	(207) 773-3191
Massachusetts	(617) 367-1313
New Jersey	(908) 238-7875
New York State	(716) 631-5282
New York State Hotline	(800) 331-0931
New York City (five boroughs)	(212) 267-6000
Rhode Island	(401) 861-0815
West Virginia	(800) 642-2670 or (304) 766-7851

To get a free copy of LVA's catalog of materials and services, call or write to the Syracuse address above. You may also want to check out LVA's website at http://archon.educ.kent.edu/LVA.

Your phone book may list your local Head Start program under "H." If not, call your city or town's education department. The number is in the blue pages of your phone book.

(V. Harlow/Community Action for Greater Middletown, Middletown, CT)

Head Start serves more than 750,000 children and their families throughout the United States. Louie Rodriguez works with two preschoolers at the Head Start program located near his school in Middletown, Connecticut.

When you call, ask for the person who coordinates volunteers. You may not get that person on the first call, because coordinators are usually quite busy. Be sure to leave a message, with your name and phone number, saying you want to find out about volunteering. Ask if you need an application form and if the coordinator can mail you one. Or you may offer to stop by and pick up the form.

If no one calls back within a few days, call again. Do not get discouraged. Persistence pays off. If you have decided on a particular place where you want to volunteer, keep at it. You may find that they accept applications only at certain times or seasons of the year.

If you can't get in right away, ask if they have a waiting list, and say you want to be on it. Be sure to follow up your calls with thank-you letters. While you're thinking of them, you want *them* to be thinking of you.

YOUR INTERVIEW

When you are interviewed, ask questions of your own. What kind of training program will you have to go through? How many training meetings a week, for how many weeks? How many teen volunteers are in the program? Is there a period of probation, and how long is it?

Let your interviewer know that you have thought about your volunteering. Make him or her aware that you want to know what you are getting into in the same sense that he or she wants to know about you.

GET A RÉSUMÉ READY

Looking for a volunteer job is like looking for a paying job. You want to make the best possible impression. Handing a résumé to your interviewer makes two points:

1. That you have been somewhere and have done something, and

2. That you know how to think about where you have been and what you have done.

On your résumé include your full name, address, age, grade in school, and school activities (e.g., Key Club, drama club, sports teams, science club, 4-H Club, publications, etc.). Be sure to include part-time jobs, from baby-sitting to delivering newspapers, from mowing lawns to shoveling snow. You want the reader of your résumé to see how well rounded you are.

WHERE TO FIND OPPORTUNITIES

(Courtesy: Patricia Heck/Club RIF, Red Mountain High School, Mesa, AZ)

A neat appearance makes a good impression when you work as a volunteer. Club RIF members Meaghan Kennedy (left) and Brandy Grant (right) pose for a picture with Clifford the dog, in front of Red Mountain High School in Mesa, Arizona.

HOW DO YOU LOOK?

Somebody once said, "You get only one chance to make a good first impression." Dress for it, in clean, freshly pressed clothing. Make sure your hands and fingernails are clean. Shampoo. If you have short hair, it should be trimmed and well combed. If you have long hair, wear it in a braid or ponytail. Make it clear you know you shouldn't come to work with your hair flying in the breeze.

DON'T WASTE YOUR TIME

"Just find out what you'll be doing," says teen volunteer Emily Hudson. "You want to make sure you're interested in it before you commit yourself. Don't do something that you aren't interested in pursuing, because it's a waste of your time more than anything else. Volunteering can be a lot of fun if you find the right spot, so I'd definitely recommend it."

GLOSSARY

Abstraction. Something not associated with any specific situation or instance.

Cognition. The act or process of knowing, including awareness and judgment.

Cognitive. Involving or related to cognition.

Curriculum. A set of courses offered by an educational institution.

E.g. An abbreviation meaning "for example".

Focus group. A research technique used to determine attitudes and opinions through discussion of a topic by a small group of people.

Fortune 500 companies. The nation's 500 largest companies, according to *Fortune,* a leading business magazine.

Functional illiteracy. The inability of an individual to use reading, speaking, writing and computational skills in everyday life situations; basic illiteracy is the inability to read or write.

Humanistic. Related to the literary culture and the study of human interests and values.

Neuron. The cell that is the basic functional unit of nervous tissue.

Orientation. Circumstance in which one becomes acquainted with the existing situation or environment.

Paraprofessional. A trained assistant to a professional person; a teacher's aide.

Probation. A period of testing and trial to determine a person's fitness for a job or for school.

Recalcitrant. Obstinately defiant of authority; unresponsive.

Remedial. Any effort (usually in a formal program) to remedy a given situation.

Résumé. A brief statement of one's experience and qualifications, presented when applying for a position.

Stymied. Prevented by some obstacle from moving, acting or thinking (originally, from the game of golf, when the ball nearer the hole lies in the path of another player's ball).

SUGGESTIONS FOR FURTHER READING

Anderson, Walter. *Read with Me.* Boston: Houghton Mifflin, 1990.

Armstrong, William H. *Study Is Hard Work.* New York: Harper, 1967.

Carruth, Gorton. *The Young Reader's Companion.* New Providence, NJ: Bowker, 1993.

Chase, Stuart. *The Tyranny of Words.* New York: Harcourt Brace Jovanovich, 1966.

Cullinan, Bernice E. *Read to Me: Raising Kids Who Love to Read.* New York: Scholastic, 1992.

Draves, William. *How to Teach Adults.* Manhattan, KS: Learning Resources Network, 1984.

Edelfelt, Roy A. *Careers in Education.* Lincolnwood, IL: VGM Career Horizons, 1992.

Fine, Janet. *Opportunities in Teaching Careers.* Lincolnwood, IL: VGM Career Horizons, 1989.

Fisher, Gary L., and R.W. Cummings. *The Survival Guide for Kids with LD (Learning Differences).* Minneapolis: Free Spirit, 1991.

Fox, Barbara. *Rx for Reading.* New York: Penguin, 1989.

Gibbons, Gail. *Check It Out: The Book About Libraries.* New York: Harcourt Brace Jovanovich, 1985.

Gordon, Charlotte. *How to Find What You Want in the Library.* Hauppage, NY: Barron's, 1978.

Hauser, Jill F. *Growing Up Reading: Learning to Read Through Creative Play.* Charlotte, VT: Williamson, 1993.

Knox, Jean M. *Learning Disabilities.* New York: Chelsea House, 1989.

Kozol, Jonathan. *On Being a Teacher.* New York: Continuum, 1981.

Leonhardt, Mary. *Keeping Kids Reading: How to Raise Avid Readers in the Video Age.* New York: Crown, 1996.

———. *99 Ways to Get Kids to Love Reading and One Hundred Books They'll Love.* New York: Crown, 1997.

———. *Parents Who Love Reading, Kids Who Don't: How It Happens and What You Can Do About It.* New York: Crown, 1993.

Macrorie, Ken. *Twenty Teachers.* New York: Oxford, 1987.

McInerney, Claire F. *Find It: The Inside Story at Your Library.* Minneapolis: Lerner, 1989.

Palonsky, Stuart B. *900 Shows a Year: A Look at Teaching from the Teacher's Side of the Desk.* New York: McGraw-Hill, 1986.

Rosenthal, Nadine. *Teach Someone to Read: A Step-by-step Guide for Literacy Tutors, Including Diagnostic Phonics and Comprehension Assessments.* Belmont, CA: Fearon Education, 1987.

Sticht, Thomas G., and Barbara A. McDonald. *Teach the Mother and Reach the Child: Literacy Across Generations.* San Diego: Applied Behavioral and Cognitive Sciences, Inc., 1990.

Zigler, Edward. *Head Start: The Inside Story of America's Most Successful Educational Experiment.* New York: Basic Books, 1992.

In the reference section of your school library or public library, be sure to find the *World Book Encyclopedia.* Read the articles on Education, Head Start, Learning, Library, Literacy, Reading and Teaching. Also check the "Other related articles" listed at the end of each.

The following books will help give you a broad understanding of volunteerism and opportunities in community service.

Berkowitz, Bill. *Local Heroes: The Rebirth of Heroism in America.* Lexington, MA: Lexington Books (D.C. Heath), 1987.

Buckley, William F., Jr. *Gratitude: Reflections on What We Owe to Our Country.* New York: Random House, 1990.

Coles, Robert. *The Call of Service: A Witness to Idealism.* Boston: Houghton Mifflin, 1993.

Daloz, Laurent A., et al. *Common Fire: Lives of Commitment in a Complex World.* Boston: Beacon Press, 1996.

Griggs, John, editor. *Simple Acts of Kindness: Volunteering in the Age of AIDS.* New York: United Hospital Fund of New York, 1989.

Luks, Allan, with Peggy Payne. *The Healing Power of Doing Good: The Health and Spiritual Benefits of Helping Others.* New York: Fawcett Columbine, 1991.

Olasky, Marvin. *Renewing American Compassion.* New York: The Free Press (Simon & Schuster), 1996.

Tarshis, Lauren. *Taking Off: Extraordinary Ways to Spend Your First Year Out of College.* New York: Fireside (Simon & Schuster), 1989.

Wuthnow, Robert. *Acts of Compassion: Caring for Others and Helping Ourselves.* Princeton, NJ: Princeton University Press, 1991.

A

affective area (of education) 12
attitude 55–56

B

behavior modification theory *see* learning
book drive *see* books, donating
books, donating 26, 76

C

The Call of the Wild (Jack London) 44
career benefits 58–61
Chain Reaction Youth Leadership Program 32–34, 64, 67–68; of Sioux Falls, S.Dak. 64; of Winston-Salem, S.C. 69–70
Children's Community School (Waterbury, Conn.) 29–30, 46, 55, 57, 76–77, 80
Club RIF (Reading Is Fundamental) 19, 24–28, 46–47, 56, 76; activities of 25–28; of Red Mountain High School (Mesa, Ariz.) 27, 28, 37, 50–51, 58, 62, 74, 78, 79. *see also* Reading Is Fundamental, Inc.; training
cognitive area (of education) 12
cognitive theory *see* learning: problem-solving theory
college applications 60–61
commitment of time 46–47, 53, 75
Constitution (U.S.) 8
Coon Rapids (Minn.) High School Communications Academy 38–39, 73
counseling *see* peer counseling
creativity 15

D

Danbury (Conn.) Public Library 23, 24, 48
Daniel Immediato *vs* Rye Neck School Board 8–9
Department of Education (U.S.) *see* Education, Department of (U.S.)
discipline, self 61–62

E

education: areas of 12–13; definition of 10–16; formal 10–13; informal 13–14; methods of learning 14–16; statistics on 12; U.S. requirements 10–12. *see also* illiteracy; learning; literacy; reading; teaching methods
Education, Department of (U.S.) 16–17
Education, State Department of (Maryland) 8
English as a Second Language 36, 38, 40, 41–43, 46, 56, 60, 63, 68, 78, 80. *see also* training
esteem, self 71

F

friends, making new 72–74
functional illiteracy *see* illiteracy

fund-raising 27, 35, 64, 66
Future Teachers of America 58–60

G

grammar 78

H

Head Start 6, 11, 30–32, 49, 84, 85; of Middletown, Conn. 59; of Waterbury, Conn. 47, 58
humanistic theory *see* learning

I

illiteracy 16–17; functional 16; statistics on 16
Immediato, Daniel 8–9
interviews 86; grooming for 87

L

Laubach Literacy Action 17, 34–36, 53, 54, 63, 66; address of 84; of Coon Rapids, Minn. 38, 72
Laubach Literacy International 68
leadership *see* peer leadership
learning: behavior modification theory 14; general rules of 15–16; humanistic theory 15; problems of 42; problem-solving theory 14–15
Lenox Hill Neighborhood House (New York, N.Y.) 49
libraries 21–24; jobs in 23–24; skills needed for 47–48. *see also* training
literacy 16–19; teaching 53–55
Literacy Volunteers of America (LVA) 17, 36–44, 46, 55–56; of Danbury, Conn. 38, 41, 53, 57, 60, 61, 65, 67, 75, 80; of Southeastern Fairfield County, Conn. 41, 46; state offices 84; of Valley Shore (Westbrook, Conn.) 43, 56, 60, 62
LVA *see* Literacy Volunteers of America

M

March of Dimes Birth Defects Foundation 33
March of Dimes Chain Reaction Youth Leadership Council *see* Chain Reaction Youth Leadership Program
Maryland State Department of Education *see* Education, State Department of (Maryland)
Meekins Middle School (Stuttgart, Ark.) 48, 66
Metro North Adult Basic Education Volunteer Center (Coon Rapids, Minn.) 63, 66, 73

N

National Honor Society 57, 60
National Literacy Hotline 84
Natural Peer Helpers 51–52, 72–74, 74; of Southbury, Conn. 34–35, 66
The New York Times 42

O

office work 44

P

pay, lack of 75
peer counseling 34–36, 51–53, 56. *see also* training
peer leadership 23–24
problem-solving theory *see* learning
psychomotor area (of education) 12–13

R

reading: definition 17–19; programs 22–28. *see also* Club RIF; Reading Buddies Program; Summer Reading Club
Reading Buddies program 26, 74
Reading Is Fundamental, Inc.: address of 83. *see also* Club RIF
recognition, gaining 72
recruiting volunteers 27
Red Mountain High School (Mesa, Ariz.) 19, 25, 37
responsibility, handling 71–72
résumés 60, 86
Richland County Public Library (Columbia, S.C.) 47
RIF (Reading Is Fundamental) *see* Club RIF
Robert's Rules of Order 64

S

school programs 24–36
stamina 45
stimulus-response *see* learning: behavior modification theory
Summer Reading Club 22–27, 48
Supreme Court (U.S.) 9

T

teachers: number of 19; responsibilities of 20
teaching methods 54–55 *see also* tutoring
time management 61–62, 76–77
training: for Club RIF (Reading Is Fundamental) 51; for English as a Second Language 54; for library work 47–48; for peer counseling 51–53
tutoring 25–26, 29–30, 48–49; continuity in 55–56; grade requirements for 49, 56–57; qualifications for 48–49; real-life example 80–82; working with adults 37–38, 40–41, 53, 55–56, 63–64, 68, 72, 77, 78; working with peers 36–37, 48–49, 53, 67; working with younger students 25–26, 29–30, 36–37, 49, 51, 53, 74, 80–82

V

Vista Volunteers 73
volunteerism: applying for positions 85–87; assessing your interest in 77–82; benefits of 58–70; and college applications 60–61; disadvantages of 75–77; distribution of 7; finding opportunities 83–85; learning from 62–64; reasons for 5–7; required for diploma 8; requirements for 45–57; satisfactions of 66–70, 71–74, 81–82; statistics on 5

W

WalkAmerica 33
Where The Wild Things Are (Maurice Sendak) 26

Y

Youth and Family Services, Inc. (Southbury, Conn.) 35–36